Students and External Readers | Staff & Research Students

The Regional City

The Regional City

An Anglo-American Discussion
of Metropolitan Planning

Edited by DEREK SENIOR

Longmans

LONGMANS, GREEN AND CO LTD
48 Grosvenor Street, London W.1
*Associated companies, branches and representatives
throughout the world*

© *The Ditchley Foundation 1966*

First published 1966

*Made and printed in Great Britain by
William Clowes and Sons, Limited, London and Beccles*

PREFACES

by Peter Self, Chairman of the Town and Country Planning Association, Frederick Gutheim, President of the Washington Center for Metropolitan Studies, and H. V. Hodson, Provost of Ditchley

In the beginning was the small town, then the big town or city, then the continuous urban area or 'conurbation'. But the urban framework has rapidly continued to become still broader and more loose-jointed, to rest on greater mobility and to entail fuller specialisation of activities. Some consider that a new environment for our civilisation, which may be called the urban region, is in the making. However this may be, the interest of planners is increasingly focused on the problems of how to guide this far-flung pattern of urban growth and what use to make of such devices as green belts, new towns, measures to influence industrial location, transport planning, land-use controls, and the regulation of urban size and density in order to create the best environment possible for rapidly multiplying populations.

The Town and Country Planning Association believed that a comparison of British and American experience on these matters might be helpful. In holding this belief they were influenced by more than the facts of common language and some common traditions. Allowing for differences in total size, both countries are highly urbanised. About two-fifths of the population of Britain, and over a third of that of the United States, live in 'millionaire' conurbations or metropolitan areas and in both countries the strongest pressures of growth are to be found at or beyond the edges of these great urban areas. Indeed, these patterns of growth are stronger and more broadly dispersed than the Census returns indicate.

However, there is a significant difference. In Britain there have been considerable efforts since the war to guide the pattern of new development through devices such as green belts and new towns and controls over industrial location. In the United States, there is now increasing interest in the possibilities of such devices, or alternatives to them. On the other hand, American urban civilisation is more prosperous and mobile, and points the way to many of the problems which will

increasingly occur in Britain. These facts suggested that an interchange of experience would be fruitful.

Planning in the United States has also been more concerned with
economic measures for influencing urban patterns, while British planning experience makes more use of direct administrative controls.
American thinkers are leading the way in devising new techniques for
understanding the processes of urban growth and the interchange of
economic and social activities in their physical setting. Among new
methods which are relevant to the planning of urban regions may be
counted the use of quantitative research and massive data-processing to
investigate the complex interrelations between land use and transportation and the demands for housing, recreational and other facilities. In
Britain the much greater use of administrative controls for such purposes
as specifying the size of urban areas and controlling the location of
manufacturing industries, and now of offices as well, also throws up
valuable experience on what planning can achieve and the difficulties
which it encounters. Behind these different approaches to regional
planning there lie, of course, rather different concepts of the desirable
extent of State action and of the ways in which its goals should be
determined and pursued. These variations in the democratic planning
process deserve as much consideration as more technical differences in
the techniques, since they affect the whole picture of what planning is
or could be trying to do. Although the problems with which planning is
concerned in the two countries are rather similar, differences in their
goals and methods are more considerable. Nobody can read this book
without asking: are the British too dogmatic and bureaucratic in
their planning theories? Are the Americans too anarchic and individualist?

The Ditchley Foundation offered to convene the conference, which
took place at Ditchley Park in Oxfordshire from 17 to 21 July 1964, as
part of the Foundation's educational programme of conferences on
subjects of mutual concern to people in Britain and the United States.
The Foundation not only acted as a most hospitable and helpful host to
the conference itself, but was also instrumental in securing the publication of this report.

The Association and the Ditchley Foundation were very fortunate in
getting the help of the Washington Center for Metropolitan Studies in
organising the conference and assembling a distinguished group of
experts from both sides of the Atlantic. Thinkers on the subject drawn
from universities and research associations were thus brought together

with professional planners and senior administrators who had practical experience of the application of planning legislation.

Mr Derek Senior, who was a participant in the conference, agreed to write up its proceedings for publication. He has not only faithfully reported the sense of our discussions, but also presented them in a way which will be intelligible and should be interesting to any reader. What the reader will find in this volume are not the final answers to the problems of planning the urban region or regional city, but rather a series of most fruitful insights into precisely what these problems are and how they might be tackled, together with contributions on the practical measures which have been taken or are contemplated in both countries. We believe that it will be stimulating reading for all who are concerned with urban and physical planning.

P. S.
F. G.

Every contemporary traveller from Britain to the United States must bring back some impression of the immense problems of large-scale planning which face the great American cities: he sees the characteristic downtown congestion, the dismal inner districts often being refurbished by giant efforts of renewal, the suburbs sprawling into the distance, the bewildering pattern of highways, bridges, flyovers and other devices for bringing motor traffic into, out of and around the central area, the blocks of publicly built apartments for the under-privileged, the everlasting pulling down and building under the spur of private enterprise and changing needs. He is aware, however dimly, of a Laocoon-like struggle with the vast forces unleashed by the automobile and the breakthrough to soaring standards of material life for more and more millions. He recalls, no doubt, the equivalent facts of his own country, and wonders whether North American experience is not a forewarning of problems as formidable in kind and as huge in scale, doomed to confront us as we catch up with the American century. He may also wonder whether experience of British pragmatic socialism in this field may not equally have something to offer by way of example, good or bad, to American thinkers and administrators.

Such, at least, had been some of my own thoughts on recent visits to America, and it was with eagerness therefore that we at Ditchley began to lay plans, in conjunction with the Town and Country Planning

Association, for an Anglo-American conference on problems of the urban region or—to use a more graphic and memorable phrase—the regional city. Without the help of the Association and of the Washington Center for Metropolitan Studies it could not have been done. We are particularly grateful to Professor Self, Mr Wyndham Thomas and Mr Gutheim for their efforts in regard to the organisation and conduct of the conference.

We also greatly appreciate the generosity of the Trustees of the A.W. Mellon Educational and Charitable Trust, who made a grant to the University of Pittsburgh towards the cost of publishing a book based on the conference's work, which the University in turn passed on to the Ditchley Foundation. Our thanks, too, are due to all those who took part in the conference and allowed Mr Senior to use their contributions as material for this book.

I hope that a study of this kind may not only be valuable to experts on both sides of the Atlantic but also prove to a wider public how much is to be learnt, both for its interest and its utility, from exchanges of British and American experience in many branches of public affairs. Of course there are differences which may prevent direct comparisons, and contrasts in constitutional and legal systems, for instance, which clearly have a sharp impact on the planning problem. But if the underlying facts or trends are the same, or parallel, these differences are often found to be in the end of secondary importance. We of the United States and Britain have a great deal to learn from each other, as indeed we have from other countries too, and in learning it we may well imbibe a larger lesson about human relations, national ideals and international comprehension.

H.V.H.

CONTENTS

The Ditchley Foundation
In collaboration with the Town and Country Planning Association

Seminar on Metropolitan Planning

17 to 21 July 1964

Participants

British

Mr Maurice Ash	Economist and Sociologist; Member of Town and Country Planning Association Executive.
Mr Walter Bor	Planning Officer, Liverpool
Sir William Hart	Clerk of the London County Council
Mr Desmond Heap	Solicitor and Comptroller, City of London Corporation
Mr J. R. James	Chief Planner, Ministry of Housing and Local Government
Mr J. D. Jones	Deputy Secretary, Ministry of Housing and Local Government
Dr N. Lichfield	Development economist and consultant
Mr D. L. Munby	Reader in Transport Economics, Nuffield College, Oxford
Professor Peter Self	Professor of Public Administration, London School of Economics and Political Science; Chairman of Town and Country Planning Association Executive.
Mr Derek Senior	Author; Member of Town and Country Planning Association Executive
Dame Evelyn Sharp	Permanent Secretary, Ministry of Housing and Local Government

Mr G. Brooke Taylor	Social Relations Officer, Dawley New Town Corporation; Member of Town and Country Planning Association Executive
Mr Wyndham Thomas	Director, Town and Country Planning Association
Mr Henry Wells	Chartered surveyor and development consultant
Professor G. P. Wibberley	Professor of Rural Economy, Wye College, University of London

United States

Mr Henry Cohen	Deputy City Administrator, New York City
Mr John W. Dyckman	Chairman, Institute of Urban and Regional Studies, University of California
Professor Donald Foley	Associate Professor of City Planning and of Architecture, University of California
Mr Frederick Gutheim	President, Washington Center for Metropolitan Studies
Mr Britton Harris	Research Co-ordinator, Pennsylvania-Jersey Transportation Study
Mr Cyril C. Herrmann	Specialist in urban and regional economics
Professor Daniel R. Mandelker	Professor of Law, Washington University
Mr Richard May	City planning consultant
Professor Chester Rapkin	Professor of City Planning, University of Pennsylvania
Mr Robert E. Simon	President, Simon Enterprises
Mr William Slayton	Commissioner, Urban Renewal Administration, Housing and Home Finance Agency
Mr Stanley Tankel	New York Regional Planning Association
Mr Louis Winnick	Program Associate, Public Affairs, The Ford Foundation

Ditchley Foundation

Mr H. V. Hodson	Provost; formerly Editor of *The Sunday Times*
Captain R. P. S. Grant, D.S.C., R.N. (Retired)	Chief Administrative Officer
Mr G. A. B. Docker	Domestic Bursar
Mr D. G. Browning	Conference and Research Secretary

1

INTRODUCTION

'The assumption behind this seminar is that the urban region represents a new form of civilisation, with its own distinctive possibilities and problems . . . It is further assumed that the urban region represents a highly significant entity for the purposes of governmental plans as these bear on the use and development of land . . . The main focus of the seminar will be on the comparison and evaluation of public policies and plans for deliberately shaping the structure and functioning of the urban region. It is from this point of view that we wish to compare trends, problems and policies in the United States and Britain; to see how far common solutions and methods are being adopted or recommended; and to learn from the experience of both countries in tackling critical planning issues.'

In these extracts from their preliminary circular, the convenors of our seminar made plain what they took to be the common ground from which any Anglo-American dialogue on the planning of the urban region must begin. They also made plain that the purpose such a dialogue must have in view was to explore, not to compose, the differences between British and American ideas as to how the regional planner should go about his task. Differences there must be, since the circumstances that condition the planner's work in Britain and America differ so widely; and ours was not a diplomatic gathering, intent on simulating a consensus by glossing over disagreements with agreed forms of words. Rather did we seek to elucidate our dissents, so that we might draw enlightenment from them. We hoped that each country's contingent, by revealing what the urban region looked like from its own side of the Atlantic, might help the other to get the measure of this emergent entity, to see it in the round, and thus to gain a better grasp of its bearing on the way ahead. We met, in short, not to convert one another, nor to pass unanimous resolutions, but to add a new dimension to our understanding of the problems created by the urban region in our respective situations.

To what extent this hope was fulfilled is a question that each participant must answer for himself. In reporting the seminar's discussions the editor has conscientiously endeavoured to maintain a 'mid-Atlantic' stance, so that British and American readers alike may benefit from the information given and the arguments deployed. Any attempt on his part to evaluate them could not pretend to do more than express one insular Englishman's personal reactions to what he found a most illuminating experience.

In matters of English usage, however, the 'mid-Atlantic' stance is often uncomfortable; and in matters of spelling, untenable. Terms peculiar to Britain or the United States have been 'translated' only where the other country's version is more self-explanatory. Where either country's version might not be fully understood in the other, the first use of the American term is followed by its British equivalent in brackets. For the sake of consistency the spelling has been anglicised throughout.

2

THE CONTEXT

At our first session, opened by Professor Peter Self and Mr Frederick Gutheim, the acceptability of the seminar's basic assumptions was demonstrated in the most convincing way possible: it went without saying. In subsequent sessions, as we examined more closely the differing contexts in which American and British planners had to operate, it became apparent that this tacit consent masked some divergences of view as to what exactly was implied in these assumptions, and more particularly as to how far public policies and plans could or should go in 'deliberately shaping the structure and functioning of the urban region'. But it also became apparent that in spite of the inevitable contrast between their methods of tackling the problems presented by this new phenomenon, British and American planners were striving for very similar goals.

More revealing, perhaps, than the differences between us were the differing views expressed as to where exactly the essential difference lay. Professor Self began by suggesting that in America, where more elaborate regional studies had been made and where a system for the training of regional planners had been developed, a great deal of thinking about regional planning had been going on, whereas in Britain there had been much less thinking but some governmental action in this field. The purpose of the seminar, as he saw it, was to relate American thinking to British practical experience. He had been particularly struck by the New York Metropolitan Regional Study, which made the assumption (strange to anyone in Britain) that governmental efforts to influence the structure of the urban region would more or less cancel one another out. It also differed from other regional studies in that it attempted to forecast not only population changes but also changes in the structure of employment and in the pattern of its distribution. He questioned the realism of this exercise and emphasised the importance of keeping plans and forecasts distinct.

Two of the main issues, as outlined by Professor Self, were: *a*) What should a regional planning and development strategy try to achieve? *b*) What sort of machinery and tools were needed for the job? As to the first, he thought it was a matter of integrating three sets of factors: economic, social and aesthetic. The economic factors were development costs, which varied according to site, area and pattern; operational costs, which varied with location; and transport costs, which varied according to pattern. The social factors were concerned with what people wanted or needed in the way of housing, services and jobs, while the aesthetic factor brought in design. When people talked about urban planning they were generally preoccupied with only one aspect of one of these factors; this was what made physical planning the most difficult, the most interesting and the most confusing form of planning there was. We had to become increasingly aware of all three sets of factors and to realise that each had its place in a regional plan or development strategy; somehow we had to manage to understand them all and relate them to one another.

On the subject of machinery and methods the important matters for consideration were: the sort of administrative mechanism required for the regional co-ordination of land-use planning with industrial location and transport, and for the relation of regional proposals to national policies; the training and recruitment of regional planners and their field of research; the use and appropriate powers of special development agencies; the control of land use and land values and the provisions to be made for objections to interference with the rights of ownership.

Mr Gutheim said Britain and America had been intellectually inter-dependent in the planning field to an extent that was remarkable in view of their different economic institutions and objectives and the different constitutional framework within which their planners had to work— not to mention what had been called 'our greatest common barrier, the English language'. These differences necessarily coloured and distinguished their approaches to the broad questions of policy involved. The American city planner admired his British counterpart's professional status, his discretionary powers, his position in the counsels of government and the confidence with which he moved; for in America everything the planner did was subject to judicial review in the courts, with the result that every self-evident point of professional judgment had to be elaborately rationalised and objectively documented.

American planning decisions tended to be market decisions 'based on how we think people will behave rather than on projections of public policy in an effort to make the economy conform to what we want it to do'. But this did not mean that American economic planners were concerned merely with trying to forecast developments in the economy: they were fundamentally interested in causality. They tried to identify economic relationships so that they could develop their thinking about economic factors into decision-making models and efforts at interpretation involving non-economic factors. As we concentrated on the question of what kind of cities we wanted, we should state our goals in terms of the real forces of today and not try to derive them from the cities with which we had been familiar.

Turning to the means by which Americans hoped to realise the kind of city they wanted, Mr Gutheim said it was not just a question of prediction but of making 'a self-fulfilling prophecy'. This must have a time-scale long enough to bring into the account some benefits in return for the efforts made in the early part of the planning period, for only when the problem was put in these terms could politicians be induced to take responsibility for long-term decisions. There must also be a top-level co-ordinating device built into the planning mechanism to make activities in various fields reinforce one another.

For a solution to the problem of breaking away from present trends and behaviour, American planners had to rely on the example of creative and imaginative people, often in private foundations, who were demonstrating the possibilities of new departures from established ways of doing things—for example, in urban-renewal projects. Such innovations were suggestive of fresh initiatives in other lines of activity. But they often ran into difficulties, he added: 'too often we try to innovate but do not succeed in overcoming the forces of inertia, tradition and established practice'.

Mr Gutheim concluded by saying that we must look at these issues not just in terms of planning for problem areas or on a city-by-city basis, but in terms of regional planning within a framework of national economic planning. Each nation must see that its goals for economic growth were consistent with its own type of economy and at the same time used all the national resources and allowed the greatest opportunities for development in every region.

Significantly it was to this question of the relationship between regional physical planning and national economic planning that the seminar confined its attention throughout the ensuing discussion. Could America be described as having a mechanism for national economic planning? Mr Gutheim conceded that neither Britain nor America was trying in this field to do anything comparable with what was happening on the continent of Europe. In particular, they were not relating the objectives of national planning to those of regional planning and development. America had agencies concerned with maintaining full employment and promoting economic growth, but they were not co-ordinated with the Economic Development Agency, which had been set up to consider individual pockets of poverty and had now scheduled two thousand economically depressed areas. The approach was not significantly different in Britain, though the yeast was at work there. Local unemployment was still treated as a relief and welfare problem; there was no framework for dealing with it in any larger development terms.

Mr Henry Wells disagreed that Britain and the United States were basically on a par, as compared with European countries, in this respect. Britain was over-populated, had very limited raw materials and was obliged to live from its exports; it had therefore been driven by necessity, like the European countries, to see that its resources were sensibly used. Machinery for this purpose, which had been running since the beginning of the war, operated a form of national economic planning, and this was the framework within which land-use planning had to fit. Other speakers observed that the British system of control over industrial location, though negative in form, was reinforced by heavy public investment and positive financial incentives to industry to go where the government wished. But Mr Henry Cohen pointed out that there was a fundamental difference between having individual policies that made an economic impact and the comprehensive national economic planning that operated in France—at least on paper.

Mr D. L. Munby thought the basic element of economic planning was acceptance of the Keynesian view that the economy was not a self-balancing mechanism and that inflation or unemployment could be avoided only through government action, including direct controls as well as monetary and fiscal measures. This view had been accepted in Britain ever since the war, but it had expressed itself in two streams of action, working with different objectives and different tools, and to some extent in different directions. One aimed at taking work to the workers to deal with the structural changes required in the British economy. The other—backed by town planners, architects, sociologists and others concerned about the failure of the market to produce ideal social conditions—had led to the development of new towns and land-use controls. The result had been an interdepartmental battle rather than a policy. Recently, however, these two approaches had been brought closer together by the change in the objective of national planning from the maintenance of an economic balance to the promotion of economic growth.

This change called for the adoption of targets and for indicative planning on the French model. People had come to realise that if you had a policy of planned growth you must also have regional plans and machinery. The Labour Party, for example, was proposing to set up a Ministry for Economic Affairs (in addition to the Treasury), which would have positive regional planning goals for the distribution of industry and population throughout the country; it would set up regional organs to link the regional offices of the Ministry of Housing, Board of Trade and Ministry of Transport and to produce regional development plans. These would take account of how the growth targets for the economy were to be broken down by industries and by regions. It was now generally accepted that the policy of dealing with the unemployment problem in the 'development areas' or 'development districts' where it arose was all wrong: what was needed was the development of large areas concentrated on growth centres, which tied in with regional planning for overspill.

Mr William Slayton regretted that America still lacked any kind of organisation for comprehensive national economic planning, such as Britain had begun to build. But Professor G. P. Wibberley thought the question of machinery was secondary: what mattered more, he suggested, was that in both Britain and America the growing disparity in economic development between one region and another was worrying the economic analysts—the people concerned with efficiency—as well as the people concerned about its social aspects. Thus the two lines of policy were coming together.

What, then, should the government do about these regional disparities in economic growth? Mr Gutheim cited the case of Poland, where it had been found that national economic planning on the Russian model was successful in promoting development in certain industrial sectors but did nothing for the regions in which these industries did not happen to be located. Obviously this was a politically impossible as well as an economically wasteful situation. A change had therefore been made to a far more regionally oriented policy, making each of over thirty regions the subject of a highly integrated economic and physical plan. These regional plans were now set in the context of a national economic plan, and to see the regional and national plans working together and strengthening each other was a uniquely exciting experience.

This gave rise to several questions. Did the integration of regional and national economic planning necessarily involve not only the promotion of growth in some regions but also its restraint in others, and was not any such restraint alien to every American instinct—economic, social or political? On what basis were conflicts between economic and land-use objectives to be reconciled in a national plan? Could the planner's competence extend beyond the physical arrangement of land use and development within the urban region, or must he be content merely to take note of economic processes at the national level?

Dr Nathaniel Lichfield suggested that a new element had been introduced with the emergence as a field of public policy of *economic development*—the deliberate stimulation of a region's economic growth—as distinct both from *economic planning* (in the sense of maintaining a country's economic balance) and from regional planning in the sense of arranging a region's land use. On the question of how to stimulate regional growth, the British were comparatively unknowledgeable, he went on; they had nothing like the T.V.A. project, in which the Americans had shown what had to be done to develop the resources of a region and to provide the wherewithal for it to live. He agreed that most planners must be basically concerned with the physical arrangement of things on the ground, but in that operation all the social and economic forces impinging on land use had to be taken into account and the relationships between them understood. Planning in America, being more oriented towards the social sciences, was less narrowly conceived than in Britain.

It was evident, in short, that neither the British nor the American contingent felt complacent about its own country's preparedness to tackle the critical planning issues raised by the emergence of the urban region. If Britain was making more progress towards getting itself organised for this task, America had more to show in the way of *ad hoc* performance; but both were far from having an operative regional planning system and still farther from getting regional land-use plans integrated with comprehensive national economic planning. It also appeared, on the other hand, that the acceptance of planned economic growth as an objective of national policy was at last resolving conflicts in this field and enabling the governmental agencies and professional interests concerned to pull together. It was on this modestly hopeful note that our first session closed.

3

THE STRUCTURE

What is an urban region? We were clearly in danger of arguing at cross-purposes if we embarked on a closer examination of the strategy and mechanism of planning for the urban region without first making sure that we were all talking about the same thing—or at least that we all knew what each of us was talking about.

No precise definition had been attempted at our first session. Professor Self and Mr Gutheim had indicated two quite different ways in which the concept of the region was to be distinguished from that of the city, but both had left undefined the basis of the distinction between region and nation—a distinction that was taken for granted throughout the subsequent discussion. 'Towns have grown into conurbations,' said Professor Self, 'and these have spilt over into wider aggregations which we may call urban regions.' Mobility lay at the root of this increase in the scale of the urban unit; but 'people hop around between urban regions'; so far as mobility was concerned, then, the whole nation was an urban region. If a sub-national urban region was to be distinguished as 'a critical entity for planning and development strategy' it must therefore be defined in terms other than mobility.

Professor Self was sure such an entity existed, but identified it only as 'a focus for bringing together a whole range of questions about how you should plan and what kind of general development strategy you should adopt'. For Mr Gutheim the starting-point was 'what kinds of cities do we want and what kinds of goals for urban development?' He went on to describe the urban region as 'not simply an overspill of the city, or a territorial unit, but a population living as an organically interrelated group of people whose jobs, economic activities, social institutions, leisure time and mobility are working together in a highly integrated fashion'. It was this unity of behaviour, he insisted, rather than the territory in which it was taking place, that was the significant thing—the thing that most distinguished the 'city' of today, in this period of affluence, leisure and dynamic growth, from the city of the nineteenth century, which was not only smaller but (as Professor Asa Briggs had shown) an inherently simpler type of organisation.

This narrowed the concept a little, but still left the question of the scale of the urban region open-ended. Granted that the explosive city of today could no longer be meaningfully defined in terms of things on the ground, such as built-up areas, and that the resulting urban region must be conceived either in terms of an integrated pattern of activities or as a focus or matrix for the consideration of the problems arising from these activities, and for the formulation of policy goals and strategies to deal with these problems—granted all this, how could the population concerned be identified and distinguished from the nation as a whole? Was it any easier to define the urban region by reference to the population concerned in its activities than by reference to the area over which these activities took place?

For that matter, how important was it that the population or the area concerned should, if it could, be so identified and distinguished? Much more important, obviously, if the object of the exercise was to prepare a physical development plan for each urban region, and to relate it to a national strategy for economic growth, than if the object were only to study the trends of change in each region and make a 'self-fulfilling prophecy' as to how they should express themselves in land use and development. It is only when the urban regions of a densely settled country are to be systematically planned by governmental agencies that it becomes unavoidably necessary to draw lines of demarcation round them, and therefore to define the urban region in terms that both set limits to its scale and enable precise (even though temporary) boundaries between one urban region and the next to be rationally justified.

Thus the attempt to find in the structure of the urban region a basis for its definition gave the seminar a fruitful opportunity to explore in greater depth the differences between British and American concepts. At its second session maximum advantage was taken of this opportunity by the authors of the opening papers, Professor Donald Foley and Mr Derek Senior, whose widely separated angles of approach to the problem threw these differences into sharp relief.

Professor Foley's paper began by setting out four questions as deserving high-priority discussion, and then went on to give his own answers. It read as follows:

1 What are the most important changes in the structure of urban regions currently under way? What are these likely to lead to?

2 How can we most meaningfully evaluate the full implications of these changes? What are their social advantages and disadvantages? What are their economic advantages and disadvantages?

3 How can we establish criteria against which to weigh alternative substantive plans and proposals for guiding the development of urban-regional structure?

4 What can American and British planners, administrators, developers and scholars learn from the experiences and ideas of the other nation?

The urban region (more commonly termed 'metropolitan region' in America) represents more than an enlarged scale of city or town, and more even than an amalgam of cities. It involves no less than a fundamental reorganisation of social and economic life so that most of such life is centred on the metropolis. In much of the United States, for example, rural communities and small towns and formerly rather independent cities have either dried up or have become caught up in a far-flung web of metropolitan-dominated relationships.

Urban regions, as they are emerging, are neither separate nor clearly definable, for they, in turn, are interlocked in an even larger urban system of amazing complexity. In the United States, at least, it no longer makes sense to try to ascertain exactly how many urban regions we have or exactly what hierarchical position each region's centre holds with respect to the larger system. The fundamental fact is that urban and non-urban can no longer be meaningfully differentiated, nor can precise geographic community boundaries be validly identified. With the revolutionary strides in communication and transportation, with industrialisation trends sweeping all activities including agriculture, with the pervasive impact of mass education and mass culture, we are becoming an urban society and our citizens are no longer simply members of this or that local community. Mobility, fluidity, interconnectedness and interpenetration, pluralistic organisational arrangements defying local or regional limits, non-stop automobility via smoothly engineered freeways (motorways), long-distance commuting (including intermetropolitan commuting by air), toll-free telephone rate structures, long-distance and frequent week ending, periodic retreats to one's second domicile—these and many other characteristics are coming to supplant traditional characterisations of community life. Violent though the emotional reactions of foreign visitors may be to what has been happening in the United States, the situation here may offer glimpses of what may yet be in store for other industrialised nations. For the revolution is on: the airport is supplanting the railway station; television is nearly universal; two- and three-car families move about in unparalleled freedom, little constrained by fixed time schedules or routes; income has risen appreciably; paid vacations and ever more comfortable retirement incomes are becoming commonplace; the American housewife

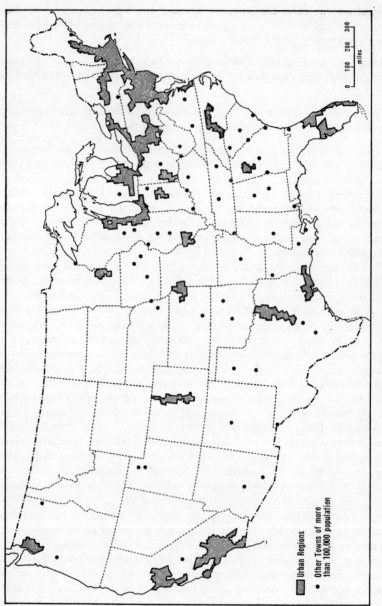

Urban Regions in the U.S.A., 1960

■ Urban Regions

• Other Towns of more
  than 100,000 population

0   100 200 300
_____
        miles

enjoys household equipment and a range of foods beyond the imagination of earlier utopian writers. Physical amenities and privileges of all sorts previously restricted to an élite minority are diffusing to an ever-widening circle.

An amazing and fortunate thing about the developments in the United States is the lively competitiveness among metropolitan centres. The older East Coast centres with their continuing importance (particularly the New York-Washington axis) are faced with countervailing metropolitan growth in other sections of the country, particularly in the West and South-West. It is fully expected that Americans will move around a great deal—in the course of completing their higher education, in their careers, in adjusting to changes in the family cycle—and intermetropolitan moves are not uncommon. Our largest formal organisations—business corporations, universities, governmental agencies, the military—often encourage long-distance moves as ordinary shifts. A growing proportion of citizens thus become national residents or, conversely, local citizens *pro tem*. They can take on or shed community allegiances as they do their mortgage commitments.

All of this mobility and footlooseness—while up to this time more characteristic of those with professional and managerial interests—is inevitably affecting the character of our communities and the symbolism attaching to community. Why, in the face of the shifts that are in fact under way, do we persist in our concern for sharply delineating community boundaries? Why do we need to argue about community size when it can undoubtedly be demonstrated that residents are not all that attached to *a* single community? The urban region provides an excellent setting for partaking of the rich and varied resources of our contemporary civilisation; within this we should perhaps learn to live with the fluidity and overlap of facility-use patterns, commuting, and social contacts.

I would argue for an approach to planning for urban-regional structure that stresses accessibility to opportunities. Every resident should have ready access to a great variety of services and contacts, the great bulk of which he will only wish to take advantage of infrequently, and many of which he will use only when emergencies so decree. I would subscribe to a policy of public responsibility for ensuring reasonable alternatives—as to what kind of employment and where, as to what kind of housing and where, as to types of stores, schools, churches, entertainment spots, etc. Particularly pivotal are full alternative modes of transportation; some may naturally prefer automobiles, and others may choose public transport. Certainly, basic physical amenities are to be maintained and enhanced as these pertain to the house and its interior and exterior spaces, to the immediate environs, to the child's world of action in the neighbourhood, and to the availability of accessible open space. It is in its capacity to provide for a full range of alternative opportunities that metropolitan living can offer great advantages.

Up to this point we have stressed features associated with affluence. We must also recognise that metropolitan regions and especially their central cities have traditionally also harboured the poor, the ethnic minority and the under-privileged of many sorts. We have failed in America to link policy designed to meet the needs of deprived persons and families with policy for guiding the physical development of large urban areas. This is seriously overdue. We have lacked a comprehensive housing policy that has aimed to provide housing for the full range of income levels and to provide this housing in sensible locations within the metropolitan region. By default, because we have not built new housing for lower and lower-middle income groups and because the stock of old housing is overwhelmingly concentrated in the older central cities, the central cities have come to house a disproportionately large share of lower-income and minority-group households. This, in turn, has contri-buted to the swelling of the suburbward movement of middle-class and upper-class residents. Criteria for the effective planning of urban regions must sensitively take into account the special needs of underprivileged population segments.

Oversimplifying, I would hope that British political leaders and planners would be willing to unravel the threads of the revolution that has been under way in America—a striking change in living style and in the organisation of urban areas. Seeking to understand what has been happening need not require an immediate judgment as to whether it is good. The mixture of American polity and economy must be taken into account; we are less socialised than Britain. Our inclination, stemming perhaps from the much earlier Jacksonian revolution, is to place confidence in the common man as consumer, and we have allowed him rather full leeway to express himself privately in the market; this, rather than a heavier reliance on 'élitist' judgments. Without dismissing the ordinary American consumer, we should understand what he has chosen to purchase with his dollars, while also taking into account the possibility that his range of choice may have been in certain ways restricted.

On the other hand American leaders cannot afford to forgo the opportu-nity to learn from Britain what can be accomplished with strong central government interest, with relatively greater socialisation and municipalisation, and with an 'élitist' commitment to providing a better environment for living. The new towns and the green belts provide case studies for American observers. The new towns represent a tremendous accomplishment, and suggest that we could be far bolder in recommending direct governmental responsibility for housing and community-building. However, I judge that attempts to fix the size and physical delineation of the new town are not essential features. Americans can also learn from the current reorganisation of London government and from the manner in which the central government has assumed responsibility for asserting the framework within which local government is to operate. The ideological adherence to local home rule in the United States must somehow be breached if we are to rationalise our approaches to metropolitan planning.

Introducing his paper, Professor Foley pointed out that by 'structure' we meant not something we observed in the outside world but a set of relationships which we ourselves imputed to it when we organised our impressions of it. In a rapidly changing world this left us open to the distinct possibility that the concepts by which we sought to make sense of external realities might be considerably out of date. Nowhere was this more clear than in the whole field of community. The metropolitan region was a large and newly evolving type of community, and in thinking about it we were in danger of being trapped by earlier conceptions of community to which we had strong emotional ties. We were in the midst of a social revolution so profound that we were having difficulty in coming up with the conceptual apparatus to comprehend what was going on.

There were several elements in this revolution, he went on. 'One of them is the disconcerting fact that we no longer have the same sort of relation between the physical form of communities and their socio-economic organisation as may well have characterised the simpler smaller communities. There have been under way certain organisational shifts, particularly in business, industry and government, reflecting vast improvements in transport and communication, which means that many of the relations that persist are no longer very tidy, nor do they tie in with our earlier conceptions of community. We want to impose a hierarchical notion of communities, which shows up, for example, in central-place theory—the idea that there are very small settlements which are served by larger centres, and these in turn look to a central capital. But what happens in a world of air freight? In the United States, for example, some firms have cut their warehouses to two or three, from which they now serve the entire nation overnight. They no longer follow the nice hierarchy which we used to think was important. What happens in an age of jet planes when it becomes far easier to move between certain of the major metropolitan areas, which have the big jet airports, than it does to move between many of the smaller ones?

'It seems to me that there is a relentless kind of change at work here, which in a sense is by-passing smaller communities, depriving them of certain functions which in an earlier period were traditionally theirs. By and large we are divorcing some of the functional relations from the previously understood physical patterns. I am not saying that communities themselves will not exist, but that physical planners have tended to be trapped by the notion that there were physical arrangements

which somehow both symbolised and served functional areas ...
Finally I would pose one last question. Given the reality of functioning
metropolitan areas and a framework that respects local self-government,
a major problem is how we can develop a guiding policy for that
local government. Last night we considered the question of how regional
plans might tie into national economic planning. I submit we ought also
to look down and see how a regional structure can provide a better
framework for local self-government.'

Mr Senior's paper read as follows:

The term 'urban region' can have many meanings. What we who have
accepted this seminar's assumptions mean by it is not the urban counterpart
of a rural region: it is that kind of urban region which represents 'a new form
of civilised life'—one which constitutes 'a highly significant entity for the purposes of physical planning', and one whose structure and functioning we
consider capable of being deliberately shaped by public policies. Is there a
geographically definable element in the complex contemporary pattern of
human settlement—or rather of human activity—that fits this specification?
I submit that there is one, and only one.

The emergence of this entity has been brought about by such trends as
increasing personal mobility, fertility, affluence and leisure, by technological
advances in industry, agriculture, transport and communications, and by the
consequent development of a mass culture. These trends have resulted in the
assimilation of urban and rural life, with townsfolk and countryfolk intent on
adding each other's satisfactions to their own: in the loosening of local ties,
the complication of social relationships and the widening of horizons; above
all, in the dispersal of homes, workplaces and everyday service facilities from
congested towns to cleaner and more spacious surroundings. But it by no
means follows that these urges will continue indefinitely to drive us in the
same directions, or that they must entail the abandonment of old pursuits.
The social changes now in progress are the outcome—whether the intended
outcome or not—of our response to the opportunities now offered us to live
fuller lives, not just a *different kind* of life.

Circumstantial differences make this important distinction more apparent
in Britain than in the United States. Because this country is so small, and
because its political capital is also its commercial and cultural capital, the
national component of our lives is well established: air transport, motorways
and the like can only marginally strengthen it. In the United States 'national
residence' has the eye-opening impact of a new phenomenon, and a correspondingly greater scope for development; the telescoping of distance has gone

much further and faster than here, but has yet to make possible a national newspaper. When this becomes a commonplace it will surely be found, there as here, that 'national residence' supplements rather than supplants the narrower habitats, and that local community allegiances need not lose value or reality merely because they have ceased to be exclusive or permanent.

Other relevant differences come to mind. Americans are more mobile, not only in the physical sense but socially and economically. They make friends more easily and are more accustomed to moving around from job to job (and to different kinds of job) as well as from place to place. We tend to stay put unless we are under great pressure or temptation to move. We are also more conservative—more disposed to make do and mend, to preserve and adapt, rather than to scrap and start afresh. And the very fact that we are twenty years behind the United States in automobility gives us a chance to see the physical consequences it can produce, to consider whether we want them, and to use accordingly the planning machinery we have to hand. These factors would tend in any case to make our metropolitan explosion less violent and its debris less far-flung. But they are also helping us, I think, to exploit more directly and economically, though much more slowly, the potentialities of the urban region for the enrichment, rather than the mere alteration, of our way of life. My own guess is that the Americans will still get there before us, but they will have had to do a lot of back-tracking on the way.

Be that as it may, the urban region as it is emerging in this country is by no means the amorphous and indefinite diffusion of activities, relationships, services and physical developments, inextricably tangled up with those of other regions, that it may seem (truly or falsely) to have become in America's Big Street. It is an organic unit, definable not only in terms of function but also geographically—as an area whose inhabitants look to, or unwittingly depend upon, a common centre for those facilities and services whose economic provision demands a user population of large but less than national proportions. It can also be identified on the ground, for all practical purposes, as the area whose inhabitants find services and facilities of this order more readily accessible in one centre than in any other. An urban region may be said to be fully developed when all such humanly provided services and facilities are available within its boundaries and so disposed in relation to its dwellings that none of its inhabitants need be deterred from using them by the time it takes to get at them.

It is true, of course, that increasing affluence is widening the range of services and facilities that can be economically provided on a local basis, or that demand no movement on the part of the user. It is also true that increasing mobility and improved communications are enabling more people in more places to take advantage of those services which only London can provide, and of those natural facilities, such as surf, ski-slopes and sunshine, for which most people must travel to other regions, if not overseas. But it by no means follows that the intermediate range of satisfaction sources is shrinking or losing its appeal. On the contrary, the opportunities that are conveniently available to you if, and only if, you live within easy reach of a centre that is equally accessible to at least half a million people are those which have been most conspicuously enriched by modern trends.

This is, indeed, precisely why these trends have caused the urban region to emerge, and why it has become so highly significant an entity. It can only be because this enrichment is appreciated so highly—more highly even than the enrichment of local and domestic life on the one hand or national life on the other—that our population movements take the shapes they do. Given the means to enjoy urban amenities elsewhere, people eagerly move out of crowded towns and cities—but not beyond the range of easy access to a regional centre. At the same time, the remoter towns and villages are losing population to places within reach of a regional centre; and where in spite of this movement the regional centre still cannot maintain a full range of sub-national facilities, the whole region is losing population to the catchment area of a centre that can. It is, of course, in the employment field that a wide choice of opportunities is most influential on population movements, but the same trends are evident among people who have retired from employment.

It should be noted that a regional centre need not be all of a piece—though it is obviously more convenient and more stimulating, other things being equal, to have as many as possible of the regional facilities requiring the consumer's personal attendance within walking distance of one another and accessible by one system of communications to people living in all parts of the region. Still less need a regional centre be embedded in the heart of a large, continuously built-up area. Indeed, where the development of an urban region is being planned from small beginnings there is clearly much to be said for ringing its centre with a motorway in a green belt, linked by radial motorways and green wedges with a surrounding cluster of towns, each with its own local centre and industrial areas. It is only by historical accident that the centres of our existing urban regions are also the central areas of large cities or conurbations. If these are to continue to serve their dual purpose in a fully motorised age they will have to export such indirect services as warehousing and wholesale marketing (as they have already exported industry) to district, suburban and out-of-town centres, together with shops and offices of the kinds that do not need regionally central locations; and this decanting process will have to go on until enough room is made for the regional centre's essential functions to be discharged without congestion. It will be an expensive process, and in some cases may have to be carried to the point where some essentially regional facilities are inconveniently far removed from the main centre; but to start afresh would be more expensive still.

A more serious disadvantage, perhaps, of the dual-purpose centre is that it obscures the real structure of the urban region, and thereby fosters both

emotional reactions against the concept at the local level and deplorable delu-
sions about it at the national level. Three million of the people living in one
urban region, whose centre happens also to be the central area of Manchester,
are every whit as dependent on that centre—for all but their everyday local
needs—as the half-million or so people of Manchester itself, but very properly
resent any suggestion that they are dependent on Manchester. By the same
token, the two-and-a-half million inhabitants of the continuously built-up
conurbation whose 'middle cut' is Manchester stand in precisely the same
relationship to the regional centre as the million other inhabitants of the
region whose homes and local communities are separated from the conurbation by green fields. Nothing is so irrelevant to the structure of the urban
region as continuous built-upness.

As Mr J. R. James said in his paper to the Town Planning Summer
School two years ago (echoing the Barlow Report of twenty-three years ago),
a continuously built-up conurbation as defined for census purposes 'cannot
be looked at separately from the life of the region it dominates; it depends
for the maintenance of its industry and commerce on workers who sleep
elsewhere, for its recreation on the green belt and open country beyond, and
for its future expansion on overspill. This is true of all conurbations: the
only valid concept is the city region which effects a marriage between the

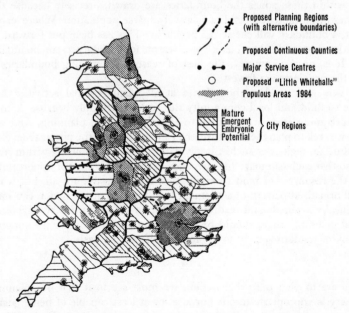

Possible future organisation of planning and local government on a city-
region basis, as suggested by Derek Senior for England and Wales.

built-up core and the area which comes under its direct social and economic influence and which is shaped and held together by its system of communications.' He identified five full-grown and six incipient city regions (or urban regions as we are calling them) in England and Wales, in addition to the grossly overgrown London region. Implicit in the strategy of the South-East Study is the deliberate development by the end of this century of six more urban regions, which would serve to cut the London region down to size. One can sketch the outlines of another six embryonic urban regions, each with a present or immediately prospective population of at least two-thirds of a million, while the remainder of England and Wales comprises half a dozen areas which are at least potential urban regions in that each has over a third of a million people depending on one common centre for such regional facilities as it enjoys.

I recognise, of course, that the boundaries separating even the full-grown regions are not exactly or immutably defined. They are zones of indifference, of varying width, whose inhabitants may look to different regional centres for different purposes; and these zones are themselves liable to shift this way and that in response to major developments of various kinds—which might even, in the very long term, cause two regions to merge into one, or one to resolve itself into two. But for the plannable future it does not greatly matter where within these zones the boundaries are drawn, precisely because they *are* zones of indifference—and of relatively sparse population. Wherever you draw it, a boundary will cut across problems. This has been put forward (by Lord Morrison and others) as a good reason for letting present boundaries stand. It is, on the contrary, the best of reasons for making boundaries go where the problems are fewest.

But why seek to draw boundaries at all when regional activities have become so fluid and local community ties so loose? Simply because definite, non-overlapping areas are essential to effective physical planning. And why should we seek to plan the structure, the functioning and the physical development of urban regions as such? Simply with the object of putting within reach of all, so that each can make his own choice, the whole range of opportunities which the resources of modern civilisation make possible for all, but which only an organised pattern of settlement based on the urban region can make economically available and readily accessible to all. Our primary purpose in regional planning, then, should be to untrammel and promote the inherent tendency of modern society to organise itself on this basis.

*

If we are to plan the urban region we must see to it that our planning machinery is appropriate to our purpose, or at least capable of being geared to it, or at any rate not ideally designed to defeat it. As Dame Evelyn Sharp has said, 'the productivity of planning depends very much on the shape of local government', and 'to get the functions of government departments rightly arranged makes an enormous difference to the whole quality and effectiveness of government'.

Four distinct functions are involved. First, the making of the national policies which find expression in the use and development of land, including the settlement of priorities for national investment. This is plainly a matter for a committee of the Cabinet, and how well that works I cannot judge. Secondly, the framing of a planning strategy to give effect to these national policies, in so far as they do find expression in land use and development, over the country as a whole. This includes the timing and location of major projects serving the whole country or involving more than one region, as well as the co-ordination of regional developments. It seems to me precisely analogous to the Treasury's broad control over the financial implementation of national policies, and I have never understood why it should not be the function of a single government department—provided that department were not also obliged to discharge by default the functions proper to urban-regional authorities. In fact we leave this function to be discharged by co-operation among the departments concerned with land-using activities—a process which, to judge by results, did not really begin until two or three years ago, but which seems to have made a promising start in the South-East Study.

The third and crucially important function is the actual making of urban-regional development plans within the framework of the national strategy laid down by the government's planning organisation. For this we have no established provision whatever. We depend on the occasional engagement of teams of private consultants, appointed *ad hoc* and *pro tem* when a region's problems get out of hand, briefed by the Ministry of Housing and counter-briefed by the local planning authorities, with no body of clients responsible for the region as such, no regional intelligence organisation and no continuing oversight of regional development. To quote Dame Evelyn again, 'planning must be a function of representative government': we have no organ of representative government at the level of the urban region.

Twenty years ago there were, in some regions, indirectly elected advisory planning committees with permanent officers or consultants, set up by the borough and district councils then responsible for development planning, whose members saw the necessity for regional plans, recognised the urban region as the significant unit for this purpose and found no difficulty, even then, in defining its extent. But these were killed by the transfer in 1947 of planning powers within the administrative counties from the county districts and municipal boroughs to the county councils, whose relations with the county borough councils—the authorities still responsible for development planning in the major population centres—are conditioned by the constant danger that urban growth will result in the extension of county borough boundaries, or in the creation of new county boroughs, at the expense of administrative county revenues.

Thus the urban region is in most cases fragmented among a number of development-planning authorities of two inherently antagonistic types, whose boundaries bear no relation (except by rare accident) to the contemporary pattern of settlement. These bodies, constituted in the paleotechnic era of eighty years ago, before the days of motor cars, telephones, electricity or any other of the factors by which the organisation of modern society is shaped, enshrine and ossify the obsolete concepts of the town as a self-contained community and of the townsman and countryman as distinct cultivars of *homo sapiens*, leading separate lives and needing facilities and services of different kinds. It is with them that the initiative lies in the planning of development within each urban region, subject only to the Ministry's right to modify their plans to make them consistent one with another and with government policy —a very different matter from the making of a regional plan. They are also responsible for the fourth essential planning function—civic and landscape design. This includes the filling in of the development plan with local policy maps and comprehensive development schemes (functions which in many places have hitherto been totally neglected), as well as the control of private development, which in the counties is usually delegated to local committees.

Professor Foley has suggested that the United States might learn from the manner in which the central government in Britain 'has assumed responsibility for asserting the framework within which local government is to operate', as opposed to America's 'ideological adherence to local home rule'. Would it were so. The responsibility in question is not, in fact, one which the central government could assume, but one which it cannot repudiate. However sacred one may hold the right of members of local communities to mind their own local business—and I yield to none in this—it is and always has been the central government's inescapable duty to see that they can do so conveniently and effectively. If the framework within which local government operates is such that they cannot, the fault lies wholly and solely with the central government, whose creature that framework was and is. If the central government fails to change that framework it *ipso facto* accepts responsibility for keeping it as it is.

Our central government has, indeed, repeatedly attempted to discharge this duty, but has allowed itself to be balked at every turn by the local authority associations, the whole purpose of whose existence is to defend the corporate interests of the members and chief officers of local councils (who in this context represent no one but themselves) in the maintenance of their respective forms of local authority. The built-in hostility between counties and boroughs, whose prosecution so largely preoccupies the attention of council members and their staffs, can be bridged over by nothing but a threat to drag local government kicking and screaming into the twentieth century.

The need for a radical reform of the structure of local government was recognised as urgent more than twenty years ago, and the Labour party got its thumping post-war majority on a platform that included acceptance of the region as the only proper unit for the top tier of local government. But the wartime Coalition agreed to do no more than set up a commission to review boundaries, on the ground that there was no prospect of getting the local authority associations to accept a structural reform in time for the new authorities to shoulder the new functions to be created by post-war legislation in the fields of planning, health and social security. In due course the commission reported that it was futile to review boundaries alone, sketched the kind of structural reform it thought was needed, and was promptly dissolved. The government announced its determination to bring in its own scheme of reform, but thought better of it—perhaps fortunately, since the Minister then responsible for local government wanted to cover the entire country with county boroughs.

The current reorganisation is the outcome of discussions initiated by the Ministry of Housing ten years ago—discussions in which local authority associations refused to join until the Minister had promised not to contemplate eliminating either the two-tier system of administrative counties and county districts or the one-tier system of county boroughs. In consequence it is, in Sir Geoffrey Crowther's words, all Lombard Street to a china orange against the achievement of the reorganisation's professed purpose—'to create authorities that will be able to tackle the problems of planning as we see them today'. The nearest approach to a top-tier authority based on the urban region that is permitted by the operative Act and Regulations is a continuous county for the built-up area of a conurbation—a unit whose boundaries, as the Registrar-General emphasised in his 1951 Census report, 'have been formed to delimit areas for statistical analysis and are not at all concerned with the way in which the boundaries of individual urban areas or groupings of areas should be determined for general administrative or local government purposes'. This, of course, stops short of the essential first step—the breaking down of obsolete barriers between town and country. Yet it only requires a one-clause amending Bill to enable the Local Government Commission to extend a continuous county to the limits of its urban region: there is still time for a central government prepared to brave howls of betrayal from the local authority associations to earn Professor Foley's premature commendation.

Meanwhile the ever-widening divergence between our local government structure and the structure of the urban region has been compelling the central government to withdraw from the local authorities, one after another, the developing services they used to be able to run, to withhold from them the new functions they ought to have been enabled to take on, and to leave unsatisfied new social needs that cry out for their attention. The consequences for the effectiveness and democratic accountability of the services already lost, and in process of being lost, to local government have in most cases been serious; for local government itself, reduced to a time-wasting absorption in petty administrative detail, they look like being catastrophic. They have already reached the point at which the central government has felt obliged to institute formal inquiries into the quality of the members and staffs of local authorities—inquiries which *The Guardian* has described as 'futile without inquiry into the authority they exercise and the administrative framework within which they exercise it'. Short of an eleventh-hour rescue from the strait-jacket of the current reorganisation, local government will soon cease to be the instrument of choice for the management of social services. By the end of this century local authorities will have joined the medieval guilds and livery companies among the picturesque survivals so colourfully advertised in American magazines by the British Travel and Holidays Association.

Is rescue possible? I think it is; but only if gatherings like this seminar succeed in dispelling a psychological block which has hitherto proved even more intractable than the vested interests of the local authority associations —namely, the obsessive conviction that a region can only be an area of the same order of size as the ten divisions of this country that are miscalled 'standard regions'. These units—'The Provinces of England'—have an administrative significance of their own. They have been found by government departments, public corporations and private bodies to be convenient for the decentralised conduct of their specialised national concerns. But such concerns are entirely different in scope and character from the functions of a multi-purpose authority elected by a regional community to serve its common needs and to promote its general welfare. A provincial bureaucracy may well be essential to the efficient exercise of a specific national function, but its organisational requirements have nothing whatever to do with the machinery of local self-government. If a national organisation feels the need to have a man in the North-West, whether to work out a provincial planning strategy or to sell a new detergent, it matters little to North-westerners whether he sets up shop in Manchester or Liverpool; but the idea that the people who live, work and have their being in the urban region whose hub is the centre of Liverpool should run their regional affairs through a council sitting in Manchester is just farcical.

The delusion became fixed during the war, when the government appointed a proconsul in each province to take charge of civil defence, and if need be to run everything. Realising that these nominated governors would be about as popular as Cromwell's major-generals, and that 'provincial' was a term of disparagement but 'regional' an OK word, the Government sought to sugar the pill by calling them 'regional commissioners'. The inevitable consequences were, first, that the word 'regional' came to stink in the nostrils of all good local democrats, and secondly that its misuse as a euphemism for 'provincial' became so ingrained in Whitehall that everyone associated with central government seems now to be psychologically inhibited from conceiving a region in any other sense.

How else, for example, can one explain the way the present Minister of Housing, Sir Keith Joseph, takes with splendid confidence the highest hurdles in the argument for reorganising county government on the basis of the urban region but persistently refuses at the last and lowest fence? Only central government, he very rightly insists, can settle the main priorities in public investment, the broad pattern for the distribution of population and employment and the national network of communications; and for this purpose it needs an increasingly alert and well-informed 'regional' organisation, in close contact with both public authorities and private interests. Agreed—it being recognised that by 'regional' he means 'standard-regional' or provincial. He is also convinced of the need for regional planning and development, but very properly maintains that government-appointed regional development agencies will not do: 'this work lies at the heart of local government', and 'local government can be a superb instrument'. If we are to have regional authorities they must be directly elected authorities; moreover, they must not be just planning authorities but multi-purpose bodies settling policies for the region across the whole field.

So far, excellent. But there is no room, the Minister goes on, to interpose an added tier between the counties and central government. Of course not; no one in their senses would suggest any such thing. The idea is that urban-regional authorities should *supersede* the county and county borough councils, leaving the more personal local government services to a reorganised second tier of sizeable boroughs in the conurbations and combined town-and-country districts elsewhere. 'But', says the Minister, 'can one really accept *areas as big as regions* [my italics] for the services now undertaken by counties?' He could not possibly ask such a question unless he were bemused by the notion that 'region' means 'province', since no urban region but London's has half the population of his Greater London County, few urban regions are as large in area as the largest of the other existing counties, and in terms of average journey time between home and administrative headquarters most urban regions are twice as compact as the counties they would replace. The Minister does in fact go on to take it for granted that in the North-West a regional council must embrace Merseyside, the Manchester conurbation and the rest of Lancashire and Cheshire, perhaps with Cumberland and Westmorland thrown in, and to point out that such a unit would lack the community of interest essential to such a body. It would indeed.

If, on the other hand, top-tier local government in the North-West were based on its four urban regions (two full-grown, one embryonic and one potential) it would mobilise the common interests which the present county boundaries negate, enable the regional communities to solve for themselves the regional planning and development problems with which successive

Ministers have been vainly wrestling for twenty years, enormously enhance the effectiveness of every other major service that is, was or should be entrusted to local democratic administration, offer able potential councillors a job worth doing and use the available high-calibre staff to good purpose. It would also focus and bring to bear the impetus for economic development which, as the government's North-East White Paper emphasises, must come from within the region, but which cannot come at all until concrete expression is given to the latent sense of regional unity.

The North-Western example may serve to demolish one other paralysing misconception—that county loyalties, outside the county hall, are inspired by the *administrative* county. They are not. County loyalties are strong and merit all respect; nowhere in England are they stronger than in Lancashire and Yorkshire. They are precisely as strong in the hearts of the three Lancastrians in every five who do not live in the administrative county, but in one or other of seventeen county boroughs, as in those of the other two, who seldom refer to their major local authority as anything but 'Preston'. Yorkshire has never been an administrative county, and not one Yorkshireman in a million thinks of his riding as his county. It is only when the boundaries and population of the administrative county more or less coincide with those of the geographical county that the county council can by a confidence trick arrogate to itself the loyalties which belong to the geographical county alone. Rutland was a county for a thousand years before it acquired a county council; it will remain a county, with all its emotional vitality unimpaired, for a thousand years after it has ceased to have one.

To illustrate his paper, Mr Senior produced a map (page 19) showing how England and Wales might be divided into nine or ten 'provinces', for the purpose of expressing national economic policies in terms of strategies for planning and development, and into thirty-odd administrative units, based on existing, emergent, embryonic or potential regional centres, for the purposes appropriate to top-tier local government, including the making of physical development plans within the framework of the strategies laid down by central government. In reply to questions he explained that the boundaries were drawn to include within each city region not only the people who commuted to its centre for specialised employment but everybody who used its services and facilities as a centre for specialised shopping, entertainment, education and so on. He recognised that the areas marked as having only 'embryonic' or 'potential' centres could not be effective city regions until their populations were large enough to sustain a full range of regional services, but he maintained that these areas already looked to the centres indicated for such regional services as they did enjoy, and that it should be a major purpose of national and regional policy to build up their populations to the necessary level.

Mr Cohen and Mr Slayton suggested that this concept implied a strong identification of people living in a centre's hinterland with the region dominated by that centre; but in America they identified themselves rather with the metropolitan centre itself. Mr Senior replied that he would not say the people living in a city region in Britain had the same sense of corporate unity as the inhabitants of a borough, but he thought they were increasingly coming to understand that they had a common interest in many things which really mattered—in the efficiency of the regional centre, in the quality of the services it provided and in the means of access to it. In this sense they did form a community and tended to get together when problems of common concern came up. Given a focus for this community of interest by the creation of an administrative unit based on the city region, he thought the sense of regional coherence would be strengthened, though it would not necessarily displace county loyalties and certainly would not affect the continuing solidarity of the smaller local community.

Professor Self said the strength of regional centres was difficult to measure, but his impression was that in many respects it was diminishing, at any rate in America: it might be the case that the eight million people living in the 'secondary conurbation' round New York City no longer went into the regional centre of Manhattan any more often than did the people of Kansas City. Nevertheless they were there because of the eight million people living in New York City itself: the relationship was there even though the people might not be aware of it. It was a subtle relationship, based on a very complicated economic pattern rather than on the old-style service centre, and it did not involve community consciousness. Mr Senior replied that the number of purposes for which people actually had to go into a centre was very small compared with the number of purposes for which they used it: they might never stir from their homes but they nevertheless depended on the services which came out to them from the centre, and which were organised in the centre because it was the most convenient place from which to get at all the rest of the region as well as the most convenient place for the rest of the region to come to.

Mr Louis Winnick pointed out that American research had gone further than British in quantifying service linkages and had found that they formed extremely complicated overlapping patterns, but with a heavy concentration in the metropolitan centres. Some linkages were now on the national scale, but this was not necessarily inconsistent with Mr Senior's pattern. His city regions need not all be of equal importance: there could be specialisation among them giving rise to differences in scale, just as in America the administrative office function had concentrated itself into a dozen centres. A similar rapid growth of headquarters offices in London could not be limited without risk of losing it to foreign capitals. Mr Senior agreed that national headquarters service employment must continue to be concentrated in the financial and commercial capital, but suggested that there was an important, though much smaller, range of administrative functions and office employments that could be established in any regional centre provided the population it served was big enough. The city regions he had mapped represented, he thought, the minimum scale at which this kind of function was viable.

Professor Foley said he would like to build upon the metropolitan regions as much as possible. He sympathised with Mr Senior's point that for certain purposes we needed a series of regional capitals that conformed with a neat hierarchical pattern and between them served the whole country. He would like to feel that this pattern would work, he said, but it depended on a radial transportation system for each centre: Britain had not yet felt the full impact of a grid system of intra-metropolitan motorways, such as Los Angeles now had, which produced a very diffuse location of activities. Metropolitan areas were becoming too intermingled to make a hierarchical pattern valid—at least in the United States.

Professor Wibberley added that the patterns of agricultural development in both countries were also cutting across regional boundaries. Farming empires, for example, were being built up on the combination of large areas of arable land in Norfolk with large areas of rough grazing in Wales and Cornwall. Mr Munby questioned whether the sparsely populated areas of Britain did look to regional centres, and whether the populous city regions were not, or should not be, polynucleated. Mr Senior argued that in Britain it was only by developing strong regional centres thirty to sixty miles apart that we could make a metropolitan range of opportunities effectively accessible to the whole of a fully motorised population. We could not afford to provide the facilities required in a larger number of centres serving smaller populations, and we could not make them effectively accessible if we concentrated them in fewer centres serving larger areas; that was the trouble in the South-

East. We should, he thought, avoid polynucleation as far as possible. Where a new regional centre was being developed it could be set in open country at the heart of a cluster of towns, and with such a layout it could serve two or three million people without giving rise to congestion. But he agreed that in an existing fully developed city region many services hitherto regarded as city-centre functions would have to be moved out of the regional centre in order to make the rest accessible and conveniently usable. This process should not, however, be carried further than was necessary to that end, because it was desirable to have as many as possible of these functions within walking distance of one another.

Mr Walter Bor supported the view that it was necessary to develop city regions as planning units, if only to solve the overspill problem. But he thought the pattern sketched by Mr Senior was oversimplified: it underestimated the overlapping and interdependence of regional centres like Liverpool and Manchester. Mr Senior's comment on these and similar objections to the 'tidiness' of his map was: 'If anybody can tell me how to plan without drawing a boundary and how to draw a boundary without being tidy, I shall be quite happy to tear my map up. If you are going to plan, and if you agree that in order to plan you must have boundaries between areas of a certain scale, what other scale is more appropriate for the purpose of regional plan-making?'

At the third session, devoted to a further exploration of the structure of the urban region, Mr Maurice Ash took up and developed Professor Foley's distinction between the external reality we observed and the concepts in terms of which we attempted to organise our impressions of it. In defining and physically delineating the urban region we did not create an external reality: we only enabled ourselves to communicate with one another about reality. Our problem, then, was to find out what in fact it was meaningful to talk about. To parcel up the whole country into units called 'city regions' was, he thought, too dogmatic: it just did not make sense to apply this term to the remote South-West of England. The rural region—based, like the urban region, on the pervasive influence of the motor-car on our daily lives—was also an increasingly meaningful idea.

What we were concerned with when we discussed the city region was a social *form*, and it was therefore in morphological terms that we must learn to discuss it. We could not begin to communicate with one another about it unless we started with an idea of the kind of region we wanted to see brought into existence. For Britain the urban region implied a nucleated pattern of development, because that was our tradition, but this did not mean that we should throw our new towns beyond the limits of the metropolitan region: rather should we use them consciously to form the metropolitan region itself. Similarly, the green belt should be conceived, not as a device for limiting the growth and spread of the city, but as part of the city's region, pervaded by its influence. When metropolitan growth had begun to make nonsense of the idea of a limiting green belt we had tried to make the idea of a surrounding region serve the same insulating function, by treating the commuting area as the city. Hence the confusion in our minds between the London region and the South-East region, which put us in grave danger of making nothing of London and nothing much of what lay beyond it.

The reason why we tended to commit such errors, Mr Ash suggested, was that British town planning practice was dominated by the physical approach of the architectural, engineering and surveying professions. The American planning tradition, by contrast, stemmed from social considerations; and social analysis was inescapably conceptual. Americans might have a real admiration for British planning as an administrative system, but it was questionable whether the British system of planning had any continuing relevance to the world in which we lived. One result of the dominance of the physical approach in Britain was that our physical achievements entered into our ideas about social relationships and made us tend to accept incuriously a stereotype of social forms. These stock ideas of the city, the town and the village had been strengthened by the tendency of social reformers to express their ideals in the traditional civic forms: e.g. the 'garden city' and 'new towns' movement. Even the argument between the devotees of big-city excitements and the advocates of towns of moderate size had been conducted in terms that assumed the existence of clear-cut civic entities endowed with corporate structures.

In addressing themselves primarily to questions of social form in terms of pattern and order, structure and shape, American planners might yet have the edge on the British. From the outside there must seem to be something increasingly ridiculous about the formulae of British planning. For example, the notion that we were divisible into townsmen and countrymen had been tenable when only stockbrokers lived the double life, but nowadays this ambivalence was shared by so high a proportion of ordinary people as to make plain nonsense of the old formula. Similarly it was a travesty of the idea of a region—a space showing some common influence—to pretend that it isolated the city and could be envisaged as a thing apart and economically detached from it. We continued to lament the spoliation of cities when we should be concerned with the possibilities for good in the creation of city regions; but because this was a new social form we seemed incapable of apprehending it.

In America there were no such inhibitions. American planning was based on a profound truth—that a town or city was not a self-governing corporate entity but a form of social environment, a by-product of innumerable social activities, and therefore had only limited scope for altering its pattern by its own initiative. This was the only base from which it was possible for us to communicate about the world we actually lived in. But Americans went too far in refusing to accept the idea of civic entities at all. Both British and American planners must recognise that civic forms could exist that yet were not corporate (let alone organic) in kind. The emergent city region was such a form: it had no spatially defined boundaries, no single centre, no monolithic skeleton of communications, but we should experience it, whether we liked it or not, because it corresponded to the increasingly complex lives we led—to the development of human personality that our technology made possible. We should look for order within it in terms of time—of day-to-day, weekly, occasional and annual activities leading us to intelligible and civilising spatial relationships.

Civilisation, Mr Ash concluded, was the continuing process of an ever fuller recognition of forms. Recognition of the city region as a non-corporate civic entity could bring unity to planning thought on both sides of the Atlantic. In Britain our success in ordering the city-regional form would depend very much on whether or not we apprehended the accident that our new towns were successful precisely because they were regional developments and not the isolated, self-contained entities originally intended.

The validity of Mr Ash's distinction between the British and American approaches was demonstrated by the American contributions to this session—most clearly of all by the fact that when they talked of the 'size' of the urban region they felt no need to specify that they meant its population, not its extent: that went without saying. With the South-East Study much in mind, they were puzzled by the equally implicit British assumption that an urban region could grow too big— that to control its size (in terms of population) was a self-evidently justified planning objective. They were at pains to make it clear that the reason why American planners made no attempt to exercise any such control was not merely—though they freely admitted the fact—that in their circumstances the attempt would be futile (and even the Russians had failed to control Moscow's growth), but that even if it could easily succeed they saw no reason to regard it as desirable.

As one American put it, 'If New York grew from its present seventeen millions to twenty-seven millions in thirty years, I cannot see why this would be a bad thing for New York'. The important thing, he insisted, was not how big (population-wise) an urban area grew but how its growth was organised; and in expatiating on this theme he went some way towards endorsing Mr Ash's views. London's green belt, he said, unlike Stockholm's, was arbitrary and illogical: it paid small regard to natural scenic and recreational features or to the need for open space to be accessible and usable. Similarly, the idea of self-contained communities was an unrealistic denial of the whole meaning of the metropolitan region and of the way people wanted to live in it.

The best region was not one where everybody could go everywhere, but one where the greatest employment opportunities for the most people existed. This called for much larger concentrations of population than the British new towns. Croydon, by contrast, fifteen minutes from the centre of London by a frequent public transport service, had the makings of a very exciting regional centre. Vällingby was another example. British planners said they wanted to counteract the impact of the motor-car and at the same time talked about a general dispersal over the country: they could not have it both ways. The very things they were afraid of might be stuck right down their throats if they rejected the city and planned development in a dispersed way.

This brought the discussion down to two fundamental issues. In the first place, the question of whether it was practicable or desirable to control the growth of an urban region's population was seen to be only one aspect of a wider question—to what extent was it practicable or desirable to interfere with the operation of the free market? On this the conflict of opinion expressed the difference between national ideologies, with minor variations of emphasis on either side of the Atlantic. The second basic issue concerned the extent to which the general use of motor vehicles had invalidated the central-place theory and its concept of a hierarchy of urban service centres. On this there was no national consensus: the author of each of the opening papers found his view most strongly disputed by one or other of his own compatriots.

Broadly speaking the American attitude to interference with the free market could be summed up as follows. The distribution of people and economic activity brought about by the free play of market forces is based on what people want; planners, therefore, should first try to understand the operation of the market, and should seek to modify it only if, and only so far as, cost-benefit studies show that a different distribution would clearly be more desirable. At the national level it is very difficult to get any real measure of the costs and benefits of alternative interregional distributions, but in America at least there is no evidence that the way in which population and economic activity are tending to distribute themselves will have any adverse effects on any particular metropolitan area. At the regional level the great need is to project and understand future employment patterns and to influence the pattern of development in such a way as to minimise journeys to work by private car.

Planning on this scale cannot be comprehensive: it must consist in the selective pursuit of strategic policies designed to reflect defined aims, to confront key issues, to have the maximum region-shaping potential and an element of predictability, and to be reasonably capable of implementation. The question of how the boundaries of a metropolitan region should be defined for planning purposes therefore just does not arise. The regional plan should attempt to control only the two key elements—regional activities and transport—that shape the region's pattern. It should comprise a map showing the location of existing and proposed functional sub-centres for employment, shopping, entertainment and other regional activities, and the layout of the regional transport system (including high-speed public transportation between the sub-centres and the main regional centre), together with a set of principles, concepts, standards and guide-lines forming the ground rules for private and local-level public decisions affecting residential communities. Only at the local level should planning decisions involve any considerable public interference with the operation of the market. On the neighbourhood scale English planning was acknowledged to be far in advance, but on the regional scale it was regarded as having failed to achieve its professed objectives largely through lack of respect for the market.

From the British point of view Mr G. Brooke Taylor maintained that the State had an obligation to create a basis for human satisfaction, and in particular for a rising standard of living. Regional planning must be knitted into market factors, but it must also give effect to national policies for economic growth and meet the demands of an increasingly affluent society over a wide field, not merely in respect of access to employment opportunities. Mr J. R. James thought the argument turned not on the availability of the facts on which to base effective plans for the control of regional growth, but on differences of judgment that were rooted in national history. Americans had not been subjected to the nineteenth-century literature of revolt against the insensate industrial city produced in Britain by an earlier population explosion. It had taken the British fifty years to put Ebenezer Howard's ideas into legislative form in the New Towns Act. The American attitude to the social responsibilities of the State in this field, conditioned as it was by the possession of twelve to fourteen acres of land per person, as compared with three-quarters of an acre in Britain, seemed hardly to have reached the stage that Britain had reached over fifty years ago. British planning must be judged in the context of the British need to conserve land rather than to exploit it, and of the British acceptance of restraints on individual freedom in the public interest. Forty years on, he thought, Americans would be wanting similar restraints for the protection of their water supplies, open spaces and freedom of movement in congested metropolitan regions. Mr Wells added that the British market needed only the slightest push from the government to induce it to take over national policies, such as the decentralisation of office employment, and give effect to them.

Mr Munby agreed that British economists had neglected the study of economic influences on the growth of cities, but argued that there were good reasons for interfering with the market in this field. One was the evident imperfection of the land market as a means of satisfying the economic demand for redevelopment in large units, and another was that the market could not truly reflect what people wanted when it had to operate within a framework of subsidies and of public services provided at average cost. Public intervention, based on adequate knowledge and understanding of current trends, was necessary to correct the diseconomies that must in these circumstances result from the free play of market forces. Mr Bor added that he simply could not understand how American planners could contemplate without misgivings a prospective increase of ten millions in the population of New York if they had any concern about what was already happening to the quality of the local environment.

On the second major issue—the effect of motorisation on service centres—it was from Mr Brooke Taylor rather than from the American participants in the discussion that support came for Professor Foley's view that the hierarchical pattern was breaking down. He maintained that we were gradually proliferating services in relation to where people lived, and that what used to be regarded as city-centre services were now available outside the cities at a higher standard than in their centres. There had been a falling-off in the growth of central-area shopping and a great expansion of suburban shopping centres. The cinema, theatre and music hall for which people once went to the city were dying, while the bulk of the population could now get a wide range of entertainment at home or in the bowling alley or dance hall—facilities which could be provided wherever they would be within reach of a population of about 200,000. There was also a tendency in Britain for distributive organisations to settle in the regional hinterland, because they found it easier to serve a conurbation from the outside, and we were experiencing something like a stampede of industry away from the centres of towns. Outdoor leisure activities, too, were taking us far away from urban centres. Our large prospective increase in population must be accommodated outside the present overcrowded urban envelopes, and one could assume that the servicing of the population would be more evenly distributed over the whole country in consequence.

He agreed with Mr Senior that a regional population of two millions should be able to sustain almost all the specialised facilities required, but he thought that to have the administrative, shopping and entertainment facilities all in one place would inevitably lead to vehicular congestion and the needless inflation of land values. The looping together of linear-type towns would make it possible to disperse these facilities over a wide area and at the same time make them accessible to the individual in a car: it would also make a public transport system more economical. He also thought the mobility of the population led inexorably to a need to plan at national level for the expansion and contraction of regions, and therefore to plan in terms of a flexible shape for the urban region.

Mr Stanley Tankel, on the other hand, took the view that the wide dispersal of urban activities had not basically altered the hierarchical pattern of activity centres. At the lowest scale of social organisation there had been no major change in the relationship between the family and its immediate environment, while at the regional scale it was a statistical fact that trips across regional boundaries (however defined) were infinitesimal in proportion to the total number of trips. The region was still a meaningful entity because trip-generating linkages declined geometrically with distance from the regional centre. He further maintained that in a metropolitan area, no matter how big it grew, people would find it easier, cheaper and more convenient to do all the things we were anxious to give them the opportunity to do—provided the metropolitan area was well designed and efficiently organised.

The inexorable movement of populations towards large metropolitan centres showed that people wanted the wider choice of jobs and other activities available there, even if in fact they availed themselves of very few such opportunities, Mr Tankel went on. The grouping of regional functions in large, diverse, densely populated centres linked with the metropolitan centre by a high-speed public transport system would make the countryside more accessible and the region less dominated by the automobile than would their dispersal over the whole country. Here Mr Bor pointed out that it was only within the city region—in Britain a comparatively small area—that dispersal was suggested.

Professor Chester Rapkin agreed that many 'central-city' functions had remained centralised in spite of the wide distribution of many of the services once thought of as exclusively the property of city centres. In the metropolitan area of Philadelphia, he said, the median journey time from home to work had increased by only two minutes over twenty years, though there had been an enormous dispersion of homes and redistribution of workplaces. We should seek out such persistent patterns, which tended to be found in the areas of ultimate human relationships such as journeys to school and to local shopping centres, and see if we could structure the pattern of development and transportation in the urban region accordingly.

4

THE STRATEGY

So far our discussions had concentrated on the structure of the urban region—in other words, on the conceptual framework in terms of which we should organise our experience of it in order that we might meaningfully talk about its evolution and purposefully plan its development. We had not formulated an agreed definition, but we had found a common language. National polarities of outlook had emerged and been related to national differences in our attitudes to government, in our approaches to planning and in the physical and institutional contexts of our work; and these had found reflection in national differences of view as to what planning at the regional level could and should aim to achieve. But it was clear that we were all thinking of the urban region as a complex of linked centres of activity with a common major focus, not as a tract of country dotted with an assortment of self-contained urban communities and wrapped round the continuously built-up area of a large city or conurbation; and that we were of one mind as to the nature of the ultimate goals that should guide our attempts to influence its physical development. Individual differences of view, cutting across the national polarities, had been expressed as to the extent to which modern technology had made it necessary, possible or desirable for activities to be dispersed from the region's major focus to sub-centres, or more widely diffused throughout the region. But no conflict of opinion had arisen as to the criteria by which alternative patterns should be judged, or as to the strategic nature of the planning by which development might be moulded to the favoured pattern.

From this base we proceeded to see how the divergences and concurrences of view arising from differences in our circumstances affected our ideas about the scope and character of the regional planning strategies we should propose and about the kind of machinery that would be needed to make them effective. Professor Self had contributed the following advance paper on the strategy of regional planning.

A *Regional strategy and planning theory*

The very title of this paper represents a revolutionary concept. Even in Britain it is only very recently (since the Abercrombie London plans of 1944, in fact) that effective regional strategies for controlling development have been formulated and applied. Today Britain is witnessing a second burst of regional planning activity, almost twenty years after the wartime and post-war group of advisory regional plans. But the whole process is very much in its infancy, as witness the few effective regional plans that have yet been produced and the limitations, in terms of aims and methods, of those that have. In the United States, regional planning seems, to the outside observer, to have not yet achieved a 'take-off'.

Why is this? One obvious reason, in both countries, is the absence of adequate governmental machinery for regional planning, which reflects the structuring of local government according to older, more localised concepts of urban community and of a pre-industrial system of judicial units that have hardened into county government. To remedy this the central government in Britain has currently assumed responsibility for regional planning, although whether it is a suitable or durable agency for the task is debatable. In the United States the long arm of the Federal Government cannot reasonably stretch that far, save by way of prompting, and the individual states have varying inclinations and capacities for the job.

Another factor, certainly in Britain, is the lack of professional planners skilled in the socio-economic techniques which regional planning requires. (In the United States there are many more such planners, but less effective planning for them to do.) But these limitations of machinery and personnel may reasonably be viewed as symptoms as much as causes. The *case* for effective regional development strategies is only beginning to be understood by even 'informed' opinion. There are many still who doubt the feasibility or fear the results of regional plans which have teeth in them; but there are ten times as many who do not understand what the concept of the urban or metropolitan region connotes, and who think of town planning as battling with essentially *local* problems of traffic, amenities, etc. And there is a reason for this situation—namely that no adequate theories of the scope, aims, and methods of regional planning yet exist that are capable of being popularised.

Reasons for this are historical. Our theoretical thinking on social issues in both Britain and America (but especially America) still leans heavily for its basic frame of reference upon the liberal individualism of the Utilitarians. They postulated two assumptions: first that the individual knows his own interest best, and second that the free pursuit of individual egoisms maximises welfare. The first belief remains a reasonable *prima facie* assumption for liberal democrats to hold. The second assumption is no longer widely held and is in fact false. But its replacement calls for a coherent theory of State action, to apply to the field in question.

This theory has been forthcoming, within limits, for economic planning. There is a consensus that the government should act as general manager of the economy, in such a way as to correct the unwanted consequences of the interplay of individual egoisms, to wit involuntary unemployment, the instabilities of the trade cycle, and excessive inequalities of capital or income: to which a further public duty has more recently been added of fostering economic growth. While lively controversy exists over the precise extent and methods of State intervention, the basic postulates are acceptable.

But no such agreed postulates exist for nationally or regionally based physical planning. Whilst our actions in this field are becoming, at any rate in Britain, increasingly collectivist, our theories remain obstinately either individualist or else non-existent. A principal reason for this is that regional planning is emerging from a background of much more localised or limited town planning objectives. These include such things as the protection of the 'character' and amenities of local districts, the improvement of residential or urban layouts, and the determination of minimum acceptable standards for housing densities, open-space provision, advertisement display, and traffic regulation.

It is a feature of such aims that they require either general regulations or rules to be uniformly applied, save perhaps for special cases, or local planning or zoning schemes which have to consider the interests of a relatively small number.

It is true that the new towns movement in Britain has always been linked with a certain view of desirable regional strategy, and also that individual new towns and comprehensive redevelopment projects represent, in both Britain and America, key elements in the *application* of regional strategies; although sometimes the big projects have preceded or ignored rather than followed a regional strategy, and the Federal grant-in-aid requirement of linking such projects with a master plan does not necessarily make the plan more than a self-conscious afterthought.

B *The basis for regional strategies*

Whatever the defects of theory, economic and social pressures are increasingly inducing tentative formulations of regional strategy, at least in Britain. Among the reasons for this development, I would stress the following:

1 *Economic efficiency* Public investment in roads, railways, airports, water, sewerage, schools, houses, open space, community facilities, etc., now substantially exceeds private investment in industry and commerce. (Public investment in industrial and commercial facilities is also substantial.) The State collectively has a considerable interest in the adoption of general development strategies which will minimise the costs of providing a given set of facilities.

2 *Social satisfaction* The ordering of the environment needs to bring an increasingly complex range of facilities within convenient reach of those seeking them. Many of these facilities are public or publicly sponsored; and for most facilities, population catchment areas and accessibility requirements can (with enough research) be specified. A regional strategy has to seek suitable general relations between three elements: the scale and spacing of communities, the location of facilities and workplaces, and the means of transportation.

3 *Space shortage* This is brought about by population increase, greater land demands for many purposes, and much-increased recreational requirements. The extent of space shortage in Britain has been much exaggerated because of agricultural and rural pressures, so that the initiation of new development patterns has been needlessly hindered. However, regional strategies need to eliminate unnecessary wastage of land, to ensure suitable space reserves for the healthy growth of each population complex, and to hold a reserve of major areas suitable for future development if population continues to grow.

4 *Urban design* This is more relevant to town or village development than to regional strategy. It is mentioned here simply because different social and aesthetic views about desirable forms of the settlement pattern account for such a large part of planning controversies. A regional strategy has to grapple with these views, at least to the extent of favouring either a more concentrated or a more dispersed pattern; of concentrating facilities in a hierarchy of centres or of accepting more diffusion; of locating major centres at the cores of dense development or (possibly) of placing them on open sites at nodal points for transportation. Views or prejudices on such matters are often deep-seated, but discussion of alternative strategies could help to reveal the possibilities and to disintegrate some hoary associations of ideas. A regional strategy could also pursue the principle of 'diversity in order', i.e. establish a general framework capable of considerable sub-variations of pattern according to taste.

This count of factors has moved beyond a review of basic pressures to considerations of desirability. Behind the analysis lies the presumption—one that is treated in other contributions—that the urban region is indeed a basic unit for planning strategy and associated governmental functions.

None of these factors points unequivocally to a definite regional strategy, and there is plenty of room for debate as to *how much* regional planning is required. Nonetheless they do suggest some directions for further explorations. These points need illustration.

c *The regional pattern*

Cost-benefit studies suggest that a systematic ordering of urban growth can produce substantial economies. Scattered, low-density development is expensive of public services and it also scatters the demand for social facilities so as to produce an uneven coverage and to reinforce the pull of a few major centres that may be distant and congested. 'Scatteration' also of course consumes the countryside which in England is valued for its character and appearance as well as for food production.

At the other extreme, high-density development is also expensive and socially unwanted (save on a limited scale), and town growth beyond a certain size increases the problems and costs of transportation. These considerations favour some form of 'cluster' approach. The cluster as a whole can be large enough to provide joint industrial services and some of the economies of concentration and linkage, broad job opportunities, and fairly specialised social and educational facilities. Most of the communities within the cluster, however, will have a fair degree of self-containment in terms of local employment and routine social requirements. By deliberate forward planning, economies can be realised in the supply of services (such as water, sewerage, roads) both to the individual communities and to the cluster considered as a whole. The cluster can also be planned so as to secure a 'green backcloth' of open land between the communities. An internal transportation system can be worked out which will secure easy access (by both private and public transport) to principal centres of employment and social facilities.

This crude sketch leaves many questions unanswered. Comprehensive planning of this type has been applied in Britain to individual new towns, but never as yet to a cluster of separate but related communities. Clearly there are many forms which such a cluster could take, and it would be silly to dogmatise about the 'best' form. Variety and experimentation are intrinsically desirable here, but more systematic knowledge and analysis would help the process.

Two critical variables are the size of the total cluster and the pattern of circulation or movement within it (and of course for certain purposes beyond it). The former depends on the totality of economic functions located within the cluster, the latter upon the distribution of these functions and the pattern of services which is planned or emerges. Analysis of these variables requires attention both to supply factors, such as the economics of different locations, and demand factors, such as the kinds and frequencies of services which are demanded and the extent to which job opportunities obtainable through longer journeys are valued. But again these supply and demand factors depend quite considerably upon *how* the cluster is initially planned—for example, upon what facilities exist locally and how easy movements are.

Accepted views of urban structure posit a hierarchy of neighbourhood, town and major or regional centre. The town may be flexibly composed, for example of scattered neighbourhoods, but it remains the basic focus for economic and social activity, in so far as there is one. But how far does this correspond to emerging social and economic requirements? Is it right to assume, as new and expanded town schemes do in Britain, that most residents can meet most of their requirements within a town (however structured) with occasional visits to some regional centre? The new towns remain considerably self-contained, but their residents are certainly more mobile than the planners originally assumed. How far will this mobility extend, and how is it affected by the size of the town and the structure of a regional cluster?

This is an important question for planning. In 1945 the optimum size for new or expanded towns was seen as about 30,000–60,000, but now it is seen as 60,000–200,000 or more. The larger the town, the better the traditional pattern of centres is likely to work; but the greater also become the traffic problems, and the Buchanan and other studies suggest a modest maximum as desirable for the motorised community. But if towns are kept to modest sizes, how much traffic will build up between neighbouring towns? Again one might ask: do people want frequent visits to a town centre, or might they prefer slightly less frequent visits to a more major centre located at some nodal point?

Urbanised Land 1958 (17·7 million population 1961)	
Existing Green Belt (840 sq. mi.)	
Proposed Green Belt (1200 sq. mi.)	

N

0 5 10 15 20
miles

The London Region.

These questions warrant considerable economic and social investigation, but they also need to be brought to earth by fresh essays in regional planning. In Britain a desirable exercise would be to assemble a strong regional planning team, who were equipped for economic and social analysis as well as being proficient in land-use and development techniques, to prepare a plan for a cluster of communities that would be based on one of the areas proposed for expansion in the South-East Study.

D *Regional strategies in Britain*

Regional strategies in Britain to date have been mainly concerned to organise dispersal from large urban areas through the creation of encircling green belts, the decongestion of inner areas, and the development of new and expanded towns. The most continuous and comprehensive attempts at regional planning have been made for the London region and the Clyde Valley region in Scotland (which contain the two largest urban areas in Britain). Recently the sphere of regional planning in each case has broadened considerably.

In the case of the London region,[1] the recent South-East Study represents a logical development of the 'Abercrombie' strategy which has been applied since the war.[2] Population within the inner urban areas of London has fallen (when compared with 1939) by more than the million people postulated by Abercrombie; eight new towns and over twenty town expansion schemes are being built (and some are nearing completion) as new points of urban and industrial growth; a substantial green belt has been statutorily defined and, considering the pressures, is warmly defended. A considerable part of the Abercrombie policies has been applied successfully.

However, the general growth of population was not foreseen by Abercrombie, nor in particular was the rapid growth of employment in offices and services in London. These pressures have somehow brought about more development within the green belt than was originally intended, have stimulated some private redevelopment of suburbs to higher densities, and have kept up residential densities in public schemes. Even so the disequilibrium between population and employment has widened rapidly, marked by an upsurge of long-distance commuting into the London area.

The South-East Study propounds a broader dispersal strategy, whereby a number of larger and more distant expansion schemes than the present new

---

1 Further discussed in J. R. James's paper. For a brief account of the Clyde Valley strategy, see R. Grieve and D. J. Robertson, *The City and the Region*. Oliver & Boyd; Edinburgh.

2 Applied because the government used, in this case, decisions based on the Abercrombie plans as a basis for guiding local planning. The long delay in reviewing Abercrombie when its assumptions became outdated, and the absence of similar techniques elsewhere in England, show the limits on *ad hoc* regional planning although its rarity (to date) has also sharpened achievement.

towns are to take the load off London. It proposes that one and a quarter millions of the envisaged twenty-year South-East population growth of three and a half millions will occur in these 'planned' schemes, most of which are located between forty and eighty miles from the capital. The Study supplements the Abercrombie concept of industrial dispersal from London with the concept of office dispersal to the larger new developments which (it hopes) will function as 'counter-magnets' to the pull of London. It does not, however, immediately propose that existing controls over industrial location (which facilitated the Abercrombie strategy) shall be extended to offices.

This brief summary points to two critical issues with which regional development strategies must reckon.

First, and most critical in the London case, is the growth of a constellation of specialised metropolitan functions, concerned with business, finance, government, arts and entertainment, transport and distribution. We have not had for the London area a study such as the New York Metropolitan Regional Survey, but clearly a detailed study of metropolitan functions, their linkages, their multiplier effects and their location possibilities is now absolutely crucial to the creation of a sound regional strategy.

In Britain the regional and national aspects of physical planning strategy converge on the London problem. London not only combines the functions of governmental, financial, business and cultural capital, and principal port and communications centre, but its leadership in all these activities is becoming still stronger. This is the consequence of the 'growth of societal scale' and the organisation of managerial functions on a broader national and international scale from key centres. As a national and international centre London has (within Britain) no rivals remotely in sight; and the consequences for further employment growth are bound to be momentous.

This situation could be tackled by a number of possible development strategies:

a) Accept the growth of metropolitan functions in the London area, but organise a 'regional city' capable of accommodating them without undue congestion while improving environmental standards. This strategy would need to build on the possibilities of a localised and partial dispersal of offices and business functions to points within thirty or forty miles of the centre. It would involve the conversion of the green belt into a large regional park, the acceptance of a great deal of urban growth just beyond this belt in the present 'new towns' ring, and great improvements in transportation and mobility (particularly along non-radial patterns) within the whole area.

b) Deliberately promote a second major national-international centre elsewhere in Britain which could be an effective alternative to London, at least for certain purposes. The logical location, given other national policies, would be in the North or Scotland. This would require a major and very difficult political decision. If the removal of Parliament and government be dismissed as fantasy, at least the strategy would require the shifting of the headquarters of public corporations and parts of the government, plus strong inducements to a sector of private firms to make the move. Planning for such a second centre is a subject in itself.

c) Accept the concentration of *headquarters* activities in and around London, but promote the maximum devolution of functions to *regional* offices of businesses and government, located in clearly defined regional centres elsewhere in Britain. (In the South-East, because of the pull of London, these would be more 'sub-regional' than 'regional'.) This strategy (the nearest to the present orthodoxy) requires the creation of a clear pattern of planning regions and very probably (to help it along) of elective regional institutions. But it seems very doubtful how far it could affect the concentration of functions in London.

d) Any of these strategies—but particularly the first and third—might be supplemented by much more dispersal of manufacturing industry from the London area. Manufacturing is increasingly mobile, and probably more capable of medium-distance dispersal (e.g. distances of 50–100 miles) than the complex of metropolitan service industries. While manufacturing is not a cause of fresh employment growth in the London conurbation, it does still account for a very large slice of existing employment. Planners ought not to assume that it is the new growth points of employment which are the easiest or most profitable to control.

The second major issue raised by the London plans is the organisation of new forms of regional development. Some of the issues here were touched on in the last section. The chief limitation in the South-East Study is that the various proposed expansion schemes are not as yet ordered into an intelligible pattern of new regional (or 'sub-regional') complexes.

The design of such complexes raises many further issues of importance. In particular, how far is the American prescription of maximising individual opportunities through maximising mobility a valid one? Personally I am sceptical about this, partly because technological and market conditions now tend to such a scattered and flexible development pattern that the values of mobility are anyhow triumphant over the old-fashioned values of beauty, dignity, and order in the environment with which the planner has traditionally been concerned. His concern with these values remains, but they entail also some conception of social cohesion even if this can no longer be incorporated in the older civic ideals. The dangers of authoritarianism in a stress on social cohesion are obvious enough, yet the need for helping the integration of divergent social currents remains very important—in relation, for example, to the opposite pressures exerted by the needs of those who are motorised and those who depend upon public transport. It is through the civilised solution of such issues rather than through complete subordination to majority counts and market trends that regional planning can prove its worth.

The first American contribution to this session came from Mr Slayton, who concentrated on the obstacles to strategic planning in the United States, and particularly on the lack of governmental machinery for planning at the regional level.

It did not in the least disturb him, he said, that British and American planners should have different approaches to the problem of controlling the growth of urban regions. Britain might end up with the green belt and the United States with green wedges or scattered open spaces. Britain might seek to limit a region's population (though not, as yet, very successfully), while America did not even talk about making any such attempt. But both had the same ends in view, and neither could tackle the problem without suitable machinery.

The framework within which planners had to operate was in some ways much more inhibiting in America than in Britain. Every American metropolitan area had a multiplicity of local government units, which competed with one another for the industries and higher-income families that brought in tax revenue without requiring much in the way of municipal services. Each of these municipalities controlled the use of land within its borders and made its own decisions on the location of parks, schools, etc., often with little regard for any regional development plan; and such was the emphasis on home rule in the United States that this situation was unlikely to be changed. The suburban municipalities also had various devices for excluding Negroes, and the resulting concentration of poor and Negro families in the centres of large cities did not augur well for the proper development of the urban region as a whole.

Another serious problem was the 'property-rights syndrome': there was a strong feeling that the owner of a piece of land should be able to use it and dispose of it as he chose. Zoning ordinances were now accepted, but the compulsory purchase of land for urban renewal—the only available means of shaping urban redevelopment—was still opposed on ideological grounds. There was also a general presumption that all new construction and rebuilding should be carried out by

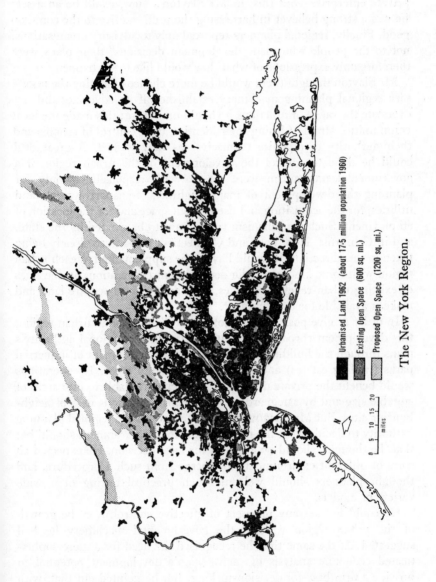

Urbanised Land 1962 (about 17·5 million population 1960)

Existing Open Space (600 sq. mi.)

Proposed Open Space (1200 sq. mi.)

The New York Region.

N

0 5 10 15 20
miles

private enterprise—but this, in Mr Slayton's view, could be an asset: he was a strong believer in harnessing the profit motive to the common good. Finally, regional planners reported only to advisory organisations, not to the people who made development decisions; their plans were therefore only expressions of what they would like to see happen.

Mr Slayton thought there would be more chance of getting the necessary regional planning machinery established if its advocates did not overstate the range of functions it should undertake; this made the local communities afraid of losing their identity, their control of schools and their authority to organise themselves as they wished. A great deal could be done to control the development of the urban region if a governmental mechanism were set up with responsibility only for planning the development of major highways, transport systems and utilities, for the acquisition and use of open space and for the location of employment. Such a mechanism would have to be created by the state, and in California, New York and Connecticut steps were already being taken in this direction. It would have to be supplemented in each urban region with some kind of public development corporation, on the lines of existing urban-renewal agencies, with authority to acquire land and make it available for development.

In order to give positive direction to the shaping of an urban region, this development corporation should carry out the regional authority's plans through the building of new towns, the development of industrial parks (trading estates) and the renewal of slum areas. Its operations would benefit the private developer by making available to him areas of suitable size and by safeguarding him against capricious uses of neighbouring sites. But Mr Slayton would not empower the regional planning authority to decide what the nature of the local environment should be: that, he thought, should be a matter for local decision. He expected all sorts of different environments to emerge from such a procedure, and thought planners should welcome such practical testing of a wide variety of models.

He could not see any prospect of effective control over the growth of the urban region without the governmental machinery he had suggested. At the same time he recognised the need for a more sophisticated economic analysis of each region's development potential to provide a firm base for decision-making. But he pointed out that, with or without an economic base, decisions were going to be made anyway.

Mr Slayton's contribution evoked some English queries and more American supplementary statements. Mr Desmond Heap said he had gathered that, apart from the 'ad-hockery' of urban-renewal projects, American planning was limited to zoning ordinances and use of the 'police power', which handed over the ultimate decisions to judges. This was town planning not by town planners but by lawyers, and speaking as a lawyer himself he disapproved of it. In Baltimore there were three urban-renewal agencies at work on different schemes, but there was nothing in the nature of an overall plan for the city, let alone the city region. Why should not the city council do the job itself?

Mr Slayton explained that *ad hoc* agencies were set up because the city's borrowing powers were limited by state legislation, but their governing boards were appointed by the mayor and their plans had to be approved by the city planning commission and city council. The main obstacle to the setting up of a regional planning organisation was the opposition of the municipalities, particularly the suburban municipalities; but in some regions elected officials representing the major cities and counties had formed associations to look at the metropolitan area as a whole and review its plans.

Professor Daniel Mandelker thought American planners exaggerated both the obstacles and the extent to which comprehensive planning was being achieved. There was a considerable potential, not yet fully appreciated, in the Federal Government's informal powers to give an impetus to planning by threatening to withhold financial aid for road-building, housing and urban renewal unless comprehensive plans were prepared and put into effect. Professor Foley added that the strength of state legislation and of co-operation among local authorities in the planning field varied widely. In California the political climate was relatively favourable for planning: much was being done by municipalities and counties, working together with strong public relations programmes, to create a receptive atmosphere within their communities; one county planning agency was providing something like a regional plan for a population of nearly a million.

Mr Slayton agreed that the Federal Government was committed to the planning process, particularly at the regional level. It helped states and metropolitan areas to the tune of some ten million dollars a year under a special Planning Assistance Programme, and this was supplemented with money put in by the Bureau of Public Roads under the Highway Planning Programme. It was a requirement of several Federal assistance programmes (including one for open space) that there should be a metropolitan plan—even though there was no machinery for it—and recent legislation made Federal subsidies to mass-transit authorities

4

within metropolitan areas conditional upon there being a metropolitan plan. The Poverty Programme, which was expected shortly to be the subject of legislation, together with the Federal commitment to national housing and urban-renewal goals, would provide mechanisms that could be used to get such plans put into effect.

The chairman of this session, Mr Winnick, more than once found it necessary to redirect the seminar's attention from the machinery by which a regional strategy could be implemented to the goals at which it should aim. Apparently there was another broad division of opinion, cutting across national lines, between what might be called the idealists and the pragmatists—between those who thought the machinery should be designed to implement a strategy based on predetermined goals, and those who saw little point in the pursuit of goals requiring a strategy for the implementation of which no machinery existed or was likely to be created. Nevertheless it proved possible to find some common ground in the exploration of a theoretical basis for regional strategy-making.

Professor Self agreed with Mr Slayton that planners must learn to understand and make use of market forces—including not only the self-interest of the private developer but also the incidence of taxes, subsidies and price regulations. He thought the main difference between the British and American planning contexts lay not in the use made of market forces, nor (as Mr James had suggested) in historical background and acreage per head, but in the degree of their willingness to make political power as well as market forces serve planning ends. Given the will, however, the problem of the way had still to be solved. Both countries, to differing extents, now accepted the view that the State should manage the economy, and there was broad agreement on the social purposes and rationale of governmental management in the economic field. But even in Britain there was no clear and systematic rationale of governmental action in the field of physical planning. We had certain agreed goals and we had certain disputed policies, but no theory to bridge the gap between the general social aims of governmental management and the actual planning of the physical environment.

One purpose of environmental management which all might agree should be included in such a rationale, he suggested, was to realise economies in development. Instead of letting private developers set the pace and requiring local authorities to follow with the provision of roads, schools, water, sewerage and other facilities, we should make planned public investment in the infrastructure of development serve as a means of getting it carried out at an economical scale, density and location. Similarly, we should encourage development to take forms that kept the journey to work short, either by making the commuter pay the marginal cost of his movements, by levying pay-roll taxes on central employment locations or by the public establishment of the actual framework of development. Where possible, it was better to allow freedom of choice and make the individual pay the social cost of uneconomic forms of development (like isolated housing in the country) rather than to impose an economical form.

Another deliberate purpose in the rationale of physical planning should be to reconcile majority and minority interests, such as the users of private and public transport. Private motoring made for a scattered pattern of facilities, whereas their concentration on densely used routes was necessary to make a public transport service pay. If the interests of the motoring majority were allowed to dominate the pattern of development, the old and the very young might lose more than the motorists gained, or there might be a tendency towards segregation by age and wealth. American planning literature laid great stress on the values of mobility and opportunity, but we should be getting these anyway. The problem was rather one of reconciling these individualistic values with the social values of harmony, order, dignity and beauty.

This raised the question of whether the development of a strong rationale of planning purposes was a matter for the politician or for the planner. Mr Slayton said that in America it was the understood function of the planner as a civil servant to present alternatives, and of elected officials and representatives to choose between them: this, he thought, was as it should be. Dr Lichfield pointed out that if the market forces or the majority interest were not to prevail automatically, somebody had to show the decision-makers how to make a rational social choice—for example, as to whether a school should be built (at the expense of child-less ratepayers) or the money spent instead on open space. No one would ever be really convinced that the right planning decisions were being taken until they were demonstrably based on a process that was accepted as producing more sensible results than the land market or the majority interest. He suggested that a social cost-benefit analysis and balance sheet might meet this need. Mr Slayton agreed that a strong rationale, accepted by the elected representatives, was necessary to gain public acceptance of any planning function.

Mr Britton Harris identified three reasons for the failure of the market mechanism to work properly in the field of physical planning. First, it was best suited to dealing with reproducible goods, not with an exhaustible resource like the land surface, on which market decisions expressing present demands could work irreversible changes that might not be to the liking of the next generation. Secondly, there were large areas of public consumption, such as open space, in which it was almost impossible to create a market: even the development of roads, railways and canals in nineteenth-century America had been a matter of public policy aimed at cementing the nation together and involving many considerations other than market-type relationships. Thirdly, 'in a sense market forces are always climbing the hill that they are on. Market forces optimise only on a local scale, and in many metropolitan areas local optima are not necessarily long-run optima. For example, local organisation would never have created the new towns. If you wish to change patterns or to introduce a new and more efficient pattern which is far removed from present conditions, you have to intervene in the market and create new centres of growth. These may later be developed by market forces but they will never be started by them.' This applied particularly to the creation in metropolitan regions of sub-centres with populations of one or two million, which might form a very efficient pattern but one that could never be initiated by market forces: it involved a very affirmative and active policy such as was not yet accepted in the United States.

Mr Gutheim referred to a report by a United States Presidential Committee, published in 1961, which attempted to define goals for an urban society. There was, he said, clear and increasingly sophisticated agreement in America on what these goals should be. They included, for example, not only a house in a pleasant neighbourhood for every family, but a mechanism to ensure that each community had built into it such a variety of types of accommodation and tenure at various rent levels that each household could satisfy its changing needs by movements within the community, instead of having to resettle itself elsewhere. It was also generally agreed that the pattern of housing should be adapted to changes in the distribution of employment centres, in order that all should have access, at a reasonable cost in time, money and effort, to a market for their services offering a choice of jobs and opportunities for advancement. A third area of general agreement was that the plan must reflect the popular demand for better schools, recreational facilities and community organisation.

But there were still differences of opinion about the extent to which planning should seek also to assure equal opportunity for people of all races and all incomes, or to contribute to such other objectives as national or regional economic growth—as well as about the extent to which it should be supported by public activity in the economic field. New town legislation, for example, was being opposed by certain cities and states because they felt their welfare and rights would be affected. On the other hand, America was becoming aware not only of pockets of poverty and of the deficiencies of the free market, but also of the dilemma of the affluent society characterised by Kenneth Galbraith in the phrase 'a picnic by a polluted stream': a Presidential Commission on Natural Beauties had now been established.

Mr Cohen said that in America the planning process was in effect a framework by which the community through its political leadership organised itself to make informed, intelligent decisions about factors affecting its future development. The planner's task had increasingly become that of perfecting this framework by getting a more acute definition of objectives and a reconciliation between contending factors and choices: hence his tendency to shy away from the statement of general goals. Those who were involved in this democratic decision-making process found it hard to explain, yet set great store by it. Their job was to contribute to a political process involving an input of professional analysis, so that the community could engage in open and free discussion about its choices and arrive at its own decisions. This was a noble aim. Professor Self, however, confessed himself appalled by the assumption that the planner was purely a technical staff man, tossing his problems to the sovereign people for decision. Admittedly he should stop short of dogmatism and should offer alternatives, but he should have his own informed opinion as to what planning should achieve and be prepared to make a positive contribution to the setting of goals.

Mr Tankel thought the real difficulty lay in the combination of conflicting goals; American planners might have some lessons to teach their British colleagues about the techniques of presenting alternative living patterns within a region to the public and getting them to formulate their own goals. Mr Wells suggested that social efficiency summed up the goals of planning at all levels, but Mr Ash contended that a rationale for planning could be found only in a concern for civic form expressed in terms of order, harmony and pattern: it could not be based on social cost-benefit analysis, as Dr Lichfield had suggested, because planning did not deal with verifiable scientific truths. He complained that the discussion had left him quite unsure about what the American contributors regarded as the pattern of a city region. Mr Gutheim assured him that he would find a very specific expression of their goals in the major projects to be discussed at a later session.

5

THE MACHINERY

This last discussion had shown that we could make only limited progress by trying to derive a rationale for the strategy of regional planning from general social and environmental goals. Yet it was equally evident that, given the accepted fact of the region's emergence as the most significant scale of activity, from the planning standpoint, in the urban civilisation of today, planning must remain a very ineffectual process if its only strategic objectives at this level were those which existing machinery enabled it to reach. The only way out of this dilemma seemed to be to regard the development of an organisation that would make regional planning practicable as itself the primary strategic objective, and meanwhile to conduct the pursuit of ulterior goals in ways that helped to make this initial goal attainable. If this were so, it followed that the planner could not insulate himself entirely from the problems of how to organise the planning process. He could not regard himself as no more than a technical staff man, objectively presenting the implications of alternative courses and disclaiming all interest in, or responsibility for, the consequences of the choice made between them. He must be, to some extent, if not a deliberate manipulator of the democratic decision-making process, at least a purposeful educator of the public opinion that conditioned its outcome. It followed, too, that it was time for our seminar to leave generalities aside and get down to the consideration of what was being done in particular urban regions to produce strategic plans on the regional scale and to create effective machinery for their implementation.

Mr Cohen, opening the fifth session, dealt with the planning process in the New York metropolitan region. His preliminary paper read as follows:

Three of the great metropolitan centres of Western industrial society—New

York, London and Paris—have in the last decade attempted significant moves to strengthen planning and decision-making at the metropolitan level. In two of these—Greater London and Grand Paris—these moves have been given a formal character, and what appear to be significant new institutions have emerged. In the New York metropolitan area, the creation of a council composed of elected officials from New York City and its environs has progressed only little beyond its initial form.

The Metropolitan Regional Council was organised in 1956 under the leadership of Mayor Robert F. Wagner of New York City with the support of key county and city officials of the governmental units surrounding New York City. The Council has been voluntary in character, both in composition and in policy determinations. It has in no way interfered with local home rule, and because of its composition has been effectively non-partisan. The MRC, by the provisions of its own charter, cannot carry out any of the functions of an operating agency.

After six years of painstaking and sensitive effort, the Council secured legislative approval in the three states authorising the localities of the region (as distinct from officials of the region) to enter into a formal arrangement to act co-operatively, and jointly to finance a secretariat. A number of communities approved the inter-local agreement, but in other communities problems developed. Charges were circulated that the proposed arrangement would lead to super-government, and that New York City would take over the suburbs. In one Connecticut suburb, a liberal Republican Selectman was defeated by a conservative Republican with Birchite support. The Selectman's support for the MRC was a key factor in his defeat. In Westchester County, despite support for MRC by the County Executive, who is a top Republican leader in the state, the MRC was defeated in the County Board of Supervisors by a combination of Democratic and Republican votes.

Because of these set-backs, some informed observers believe that this major effort to organise regional co-operation in New York has lost its thrust.

Greater London and Grand Paris have come about because of significant action taken at the national level. Equivalent action could not be attempted by the national government in the United States. The closest equivalent we have, which is not a close one, would be Federal ratification of an inter-state compact developed by, and agreed to by, the three states. But the Federal Government is not without resources in strengthening efforts at improved regional planning. It has become a very important factor in local regional planning by virtue of the growing dependence of the localities on Federal financial support. I will discuss some possibilities for an enhanced Federal role later.

The difficulties in achieving regional planning in the United States also come from the character of that other crucial unit in the American system, the state. In those places where metropolitan areas fall largely within the confines of a single state, the states can perform an important, even creative, role in fostering intergovernmental co-operation among localities. Elsewhere, where metropolitan areas blanket important portions of several states, the state boundaries can become serious barriers to local co-operation. In an Institute held in New York several years ago dealing with state planning, it became quickly clear that with respect to the role of the state in metropolitan planning we in New York had no common viewpoint with our professional colleagues from California. In the latter state, the two main metropolitan areas, Los Angeles and San Francisco, fall entirely within the borders of California. In New York, of course, the situation is entirely different.

Organising the metropolitan area is but a special case in the age-old effort to accommodate common objectives and action with a wide range of separate and independent objectives and actions. On many issues, the centrifugal forces lead to an atomisation of decision-making. Both in theory and in practice, the decentralisation of decision-making can yield many benefits: it provides opportunities for greater freedom, for greater creativeness and innovation, and often greater productivity. We also know, however, that it can sometimes be appallingly wasteful, and that for many the promise of freedom may be only a fiction; no more than a pathway to poverty and exploitation. These philosophical issues go deep. They underlie many controversies over the extension of governmental responsibility to new areas of activity and to the creation of new governmental instruments that alter the existing balance of power, even when these actions are proposed in the interest of simplifying and rationalising the decision-making process.

On the metropolitan level in an area such as the New York-New Jersey-Connecticut metropolitan area, these tendencies or resistances make comprehensive planning of land use and transportation difficult; they also frustrate efforts to re-orient the existing structure of revenue sources. Only the occasional crisis or catastrophe brings about action, for it compels, even though fleetingly, enough people and groups to coalesce behind some form of action.

In a metropolitan society such as this, with the centrifugal forces pulling outward and with the atomisation of decision-making frustrating even relatively simple efforts at regional co-ordination and planning, how is responsible and administrative leadership to be enabled to be more effective?

Political leadership is rarely capable of acting effectively in the absence of a broad community consensus around certain issues, but it can play a crucial role in forging and giving expression to such a consensus by awakening latent support through ability to command the media of communications. But political leadership cannot force a community to act when the community resistance is substantial.

Consensus implies not only wide agreement on a given matter, but also a sense of high priority. Unless the priority is high, the issue widely agreed on will give way to other issues and interests on which agreement is not so wide but about which people feel more deeply. For example, we may all agree that a beautiful city is desirable. What, however, are people willing to pay in other ways to achieve a beautiful environment? What are they willing to give up in order to live in greater amenity?

In the absence of a high-priority consensus, political leadership turns to cope with other issues on which there appears to be greater urgency. Political leaders must be seen as beleaguered from many quarters, pressured from all sides on many issues. They must deal with what is most important as defined by the public.

How do we relate the issues being defined as important by the public to the broad concepts involved in planning? How do we relate the pressure for highway relief, which multiplies a hundredfold on a hot sunny afternoon on the roads leading from Jones Beach, to the need for a comprehensive transportation plan for 1985? How do we relate the intense concern of Puerto Rican mothers over rats to the broad urban-renewal plans we are drafting and implementing? How are Negroes in the northern and western cities of the United States, striving for equal opportunity with all sorts of political action, to relate themselves to the usual components of the metropolitan plan? Political leadership must respond to these specific pressures from the irate motorist, the Puerto Rican mother and the Negro in revolt. There are fewer votes involved in the incantations of planners.

Another related factor which blocks action on regional planning derives from the subtle elements which go into the development of group identity. People identify with a large number of reference groups—with neighbourhood groups, such as school groups and home-owners' associations; and with others, such as trade unions, merchants' associations, and ethnic and racial groups. People tend to identify with and develop loyalty to their neighbourhood, their city, their country. But most people do not think of the region as the level at which to seek the solution of problems. They think of problems in discrete terms—transportation, recreation, housing, etc.—and more often than not they think of them in local rather than regional terms. Until the region is established as a significant point of reference, efforts to act effectively through this higher level of affairs will remain an abstraction.

The basic tendencies in our political system and institutions towards separatism and the atomisation of decision-making, which work against the establishment of strong central planning and co-ordination efforts, cannot be overcome by willing them to disappear, by rhetoric, or by regarding them as the product of inferior and short-sighted men. To achieve more effective urban-regional planning will require expanded efforts to obtain a deeper consensus around selected regional objectives. It will require a strategy for developing greater identification of people with the urban regions in which they reside, even if temporarily. Finally it will require still more imaginative development of the Federal role.

New institutions rarely arise fully formed. There are various stages through which a new integrating force is shaped. Perhaps we should be thinking at this point not of a single new entity—a regional planning or governing body —but rather of a number of new, somewhat more specialised or narrow groups all directed to heightening concern and interest in regional affairs and expanding knowledge about regional problems. For example, why not encourage the development of regional cultural groups, rather than ones based on cities or states? Why not encourage the development of regional assemblies composed of prominent individuals, including public officials, for discussion and debate on regional problems? Assemblies such as this need have no binding effect. Why not a regional economic council, a regional council on human resources development, a regional council on aesthetics, among others? Why not establish more effective intellectual and research institutions with regional perspectives?

Harvey Perloff and I, in a report prepared for the Regional Plan Association of New York, have proposed the establishment of a Council of Fund-Granting Agencies (including governments) with a small staff. This body would, first, review overall needs for public and private investment in research and policy development and in educational activities to meet manpower requirements for planning and administrative purposes in the region; second, recommend to council members specific projects and programmes to meet these needs; and third, attempt to arrange joint financing where appropriate.

There are already successful precedents in other areas for such a development. It is our hope that through this device a larger share than at present of the philanthropic and government dollar would be spent on strengthening education, research and policy analysis in regional affairs.

Through a series of new devices such as these we would be building up a consensus on the region as a unit for policy analysis and decision-making. Broad agreement might be reached on some objectives for regional development, and perhaps a new identification of people with the region as an entity would slowly be aroused.

The speed and intensity with which the Federal role in urban affairs has developed demonstrates, despite many shortcomings, the flexibility and responsiveness of the Federal system. Much more can be done to evolve the Federal Government's role as a unifier in the urban regions of the United States. The rights of the states, even though already somewhat tarnished, will have to be respected. The principle of local home rule will also have to be respected. But even with these constraints, the Federal role as financier, honest broker, standard setter and facilitator can be employed to stimulate developments in urban regions far beyond anything we now even dream of.

The Federal investment in the urban regions of the nation is now substantial and will grow. These investments include lending programmes, expenditures for a large number of grant-in-aid programmes and demonstration projects, contracts particularly in the area of national defence, and direct expenditures—for example, for post offices and for the operation of regional offices of many Federal departments and bureaux. These programmes and expenditures, and the policies on which they are based, have an impact— direct and indirect—on the development of the urban regions of the country. They may not be the most important single factor in local development, but the cumulative impact of many of the programmes is substantial.

I would like to see the President of the United States undertake a comprehensive survey of the development impact of these expenditures, urban region by urban region. Some studies like this have been done, but mainly in specialised fields.

As a start, the Federal Bureau of the Budget should develop a compilation of expenditures of all Federal programmes and related data in a selected number of urban regions. Under the chairmanship of the Director of the Budget or some other high official named by the President, a series of working committees should be set up to carry out impact studies in several specialised fields. There might be, for example, a committee on regional economic impact, chaired by the Chairman of the Council of Economic Advisers; a committee to study the impact on regional physical development, chaired by the Administrator of the Housing and Home Finance Agency; and a committee to study the impact on human resources development within urban regions, under the chairmanship of the Secretary of Health, Education and Welfare or the Secretary of Labour. Each committee would include representatives from appropriate Federal agencies, both from the Washington offices and from field offices. In addition, within each urban region selected for analysis there should be established committees including state and local officials, and perhaps representatives of various interest groups. The local committees would assist in collecting information on the developmental impact of various Federal programmes. Such an effort, though limited to a review of the impact of Federal expenditures on urban regions, would have an integrative effect on developments within the regions themselves.

I do not expect with these approaches to secure for modern times a new form of city-state or region-state. I would, however, hope that we could secure enough effectiveness to permit the fuller blossoming of this urban-regional civilisation we are concerned with—a civilisation that would, while assuring economic security to its inhabitants, permit them opportunities for fuller, healthier and saner personal and collective achievement.

In reply to a question, Mr Cohen explained that by 'impact study' he meant an assessment of the extent to which the total Federal input into a region had affected various aspects of its economic, physical and social development, with a view to pin-pointing gaps in the programme, defects in co-ordination and inefficiencies in effort. He made it plain, when he came to relate his paper to our earlier discussions, that in the American context the first objective of any regional strategy must be to create a climate of opinion in which regional planning might become a practical proposition. What mattered at this stage was not so much the substance of a regional plan as the extent to which it helped to make regional planning an operative process.

'The development of a framework for formulating policies and organising action within an urban community is a very crucial task in a democratic society,' he went on. 'It is likely that the suburban areas of a metropolitan region in many parts of the United States are going to resist being pulled into the vortex of metropolitan planning activities because of anxieties arising out of the present thrust for expanded civil rights for minorities. The suburban enclaves, of which we have many, become citadels of protection against these vast overriding forces. Where minority groups of different income levels have entered suburban communities there have been considerable stresses and strains; people in Britain who appreciate the soul-searching which we in the United States are going through on this issue must realise that it will have impacts far beyond what one might think would be affected by it.

'One such effect is that the steps which we in the United States have taken in the direction of regional planning within a governmental framework have had to be very delicate and tentative, and even so we have encountered great difficulties. One of the interesting elements about the development of activity in New York to organise regional co-operation, which had considerable political support from both parties at the local level, was the Birchite opposition to it. This was part of a national pattern. The fear of control by big government comes down from the national level to the urban centres. The tendencies that exist within our society and governmental system in the direction of home rule can, at their very worst, be such that efforts to deal with metropolitan problems must always proceed in so careful and tentative a manner that they do not arouse latent anxieties about more comprehensive governmental systems for co-ordination and control.

'In this context, the issue of how one gets enough of a consensus in a region to support minimal levels of co-operation is as important as a strategy for achieving particular objectives. How does one develop a process for formulating policies and carrying out action over areas which involve many local government units? This is a political task of the first order. One can gradually begin to build up institutions which will start people thinking about the region as one level at which the problem must be dealt with—not as the only level, but as an important organising level to think about.

'In order to develop group identity and to start people talking in regional terms, we must involve the opinion-leaders and intellectuals in talking about different regional issues including problems with which physical planners do not usually deal.

'Mr Slayton indicated the arsenal of tools available to the Federal Government; I think in certain respects he still understates it. The Federal Government has a great array of devices to influence local action—standard-setting, grant-in-aid programmes, financing demonstration projects, lending programmes, national defence programmes. It has already done much to stimulate the pulling together of ideas within certain metropolitan areas by withholding funds if certain things are not done. We need to think up more ways by which the Federal Government can influence metropolitan regional activity without upsetting the balance of power in terms of our traditional concepts of state government and principles of local home rule.'

Mr J. D. Jones then dealt with the British machinery for planning in urban regions. His preliminary paper read as follows:

Local planning

The system of land-use planning that we now have was introduced in 1947. The financial structure (the provisions for compensation and betterment) were, of course, drastically modified in the Planning Acts of the 1950s. But the system of development plans and development control established in 1947 has survived virtually unchanged. The chief characteristics of the system differ markedly from the American pattern.

First, it is a highly centralised system. The Minister of Town and Country Planning Act 1943 (which is still the operative Act, despite the changes in Ministerial titles) made the new Minister responsible for 'securing consistency and continuity in the framing and execution of a national policy with respect to the use and development of land throughout England and Wales'. The 1947 Act, by transferring planning functions from district councils to county councils, reduced the number of local planning authorities from some 1,400 to 145, thus very greatly facilitating Ministerial control. The Act required all local development plans, and later amendments to them, to be submitted to the Minister for approval. It also made the Minister the appellate authority for all aspects of development control, and the confirming authority for the exercise by local planning authorities of the powers of compulsory land acquisition and comprehensive redevelopment. These powers and duties the Minister still retains and exercises actively.

Second, the system is comprehensive. Development plans have to be prepared for the whole country; virtually every type of development and change in land use is brought within the ambit of control, and the same powers of development control extend to all local planning authorities. There is no question of local option or local legislation.

Third, the system is largely discretionary. The powers of control are not systematised in a formal structure such as a zoning ordinance (which was very much the pattern of the pre-war planning system). Subject only to the broad framework of the development plan (which itself confers no development rights) the local planning authorities (county councils and county boroughs) have discretion in the exercise of their powers of development control. Discretionary power, which the American system strives to exclude, is the basis of the British system.

The 1947 Act, together with the other post-war planning legislation (New Towns Act, etc.), ensured, as it then seemed, the Minister's dominance as the central planning authority and provided him with adequate powers of initiative and intervention in local planning. It was assumed that the new system would enable the Minister to take whatever initiative he wished and to secure full compliance of local plans with national and regional objectives. It was a reasonable assumption at the time, when the 1947 system was compared with that of 1932. But experience has shown that detailed control of local plans does not necessarily ensure effective regional and national planning. That does not mean that there could be effective regional and national planning without such a system of land-use planning and development control at the local level. But the springs of action lie elsewhere.

Regional planning

The conception of a plan for a region is not a new one in this country—early post-war examples include the Abercrombie Plan for Greater London, which after examination by the government, was taken as a guide in the preparation of the development plans of the planning authorities in the London area. But these plans were prepared outside local and central government and were advisory in character.

In the last three years, however, the government—without any change in the legislative framework—has itself entered directly into the field of regional planning, and three regional studies, of very different characters, have already been published. Five others are now under way. When these have been finished, regional studies prepared by central government will cover the greater part of the country.

These studies were undertaken by the government because urgent problems had arisen—rapid population growth, land shortage in some areas, unemployment in others—which could not be ignored. They were problems of such a character that their analysis and the solutions lay beyond the scope of any single local planning authority. They raised questions of national investment and employment policy; and some of the most important issues—e.g., the determination where the surplus population of the towns should be provided for—would have led to conflict, rather than agreement, if they had been tackled by a regional grouping of local authorities.

These problems and this new activity have led to suggestions for the setting up of some form of regional planning organisation, regional advisory bodies, or even regional government. There are obvious arguments for this—the remoteness of Whitehall, the need for local knowledge, the importance of local consultation and participation in the preparation of a regional plan. The setting up of regional bodies with plan-making or executive powers would, however, raise formidable difficulties. At bottom these difficulties stem from the doubt to what extent there is room, in Britain, for genuine regionalism. There is need for regional planning; but it is difficult to divorce this from national policies for the distribution of employment and for communications and investment. Different parts of the country need, from time to time, different degrees of stimulus or of restraint from central government; but this is a shifting pattern and does not seem, in itself, an adequate basis for a representative regional organisation. Meanwhile government in Britain is, historically, divided between a strongly centralised government in Westminster and a deeply rooted system of local government. It would not be realistic to think in terms of material reduction in the powers of central government or to think in terms of substituting regional government for local, though the government is engaged on a reorganisation of local government designed to produce larger units and to reduce the number of local authorities. So any regional organisation independent of central government would in practice be an additional tier; and it must be very doubtful whether there is room for this.

Future developments

In practical terms, the most likely development over the next few years appears to be a narrowing of the gap between central and local government, on the one hand by the strengthening and reorganisation of local government into units which will be able to deal more effectively with the larger planning problems, and on the other by strengthening the representation of central government in the regions.

On the local government side, reorganisation in London will start to make its impact when the Greater London Council becomes operational next year

(1965). There will then, for the first time, be a local authority able to examine the main planning problems of London as a whole—housing land, overspill, traffic—and to settle the main lines of policy for the development plans for the boroughs. It may be argued that the council should cover an even wider area—the whole metropolitan region, with a radius of thirty to forty miles from the centre, which is strongly influenced by the housing demands and the employment pull of the conurbation. But the setting up of the Greater London Council is, in any event, a big advance.

In the provinces, the Local Government Commission is steadily working its way around the country; and its operations will make for stronger local planning authorities in two ways. First, boundary adjustments and amalgamations of areas will produce larger units with greater resources of money and qualified staff—units which will correspond more closely with the realities of development, freed in the main from boundary anomalies that are such a potent source of dispute and suspicion. Secondly, in the special review areas formed by the main conurbations, the Commission is able to propose structural changes that will provide for the planning of these areas looked at as a whole.

With central government, it is likely to be a question of strengthening and enlarging the representation in the regions of the departments concerned with regional planning. Most already have offices at various regional centres. The Ministry of Housing and Local Government has for some years managed without regional offices, preferring to develop close contacts between the local authorities and headquarters; but with the accelerated drive for slum clearance in the north, and with the emergence of regional planning, the Ministry has now re-established regional offices in Manchester and Newcastle—the latter being closely concerned with the implementation of the North-East plan. Other regional offices are likely to follow as it becomes possible to staff them.

The existing regional organisation of central government was not, of course, designed with regional planning in mind. In part, it is a relic of war-time needs; in part it has been built up to serve the day-to-day and differing needs of the various departments. To be effective for regional planning and development, more co-ordination of activities and boundaries will be needed. It will also be necessary to consider whether the present administrative regions are the right size and shape for regional planning purposes, and what should be the division of activities between departmental headquarters and the regions. Experience so far suggests that the formulation of regional plans is best done in London (though with close regional contacts during the process); and that implementation and review is best directed from the region.

One of the elements in regional planning that needs further thought is how best to bring in local interests other than the local authorities—employers, trade unions, farmers, transport undertakers, public utilities, universities,

5

organisations representing local interests of one sort or another. So far, consultation with such bodies as these has been carried out informally at the early stages of plan-making. There may be a case for more regular consultative machinery, though in the biggest regions this presents practical difficulties.

Finally, the formal relationship of regional plans to 'local' development plans needs looking at. The type and form of these development plans in any case need examination—for quite different reasons—and in the course of this review (which is already in hand) the connection between the regional and the 'local' plans is one of the questions being considered.

Introducing his paper, Mr Jones said:

I am not concerned to discuss the merits of our current regional plans but to describe the machinery which has been used for doing them and what I think is the right machinery for doing the next lot. These plans have been only a start in a very wide process, the first essays in a new field, and the question is whether we are going the right way about it. There are two aspects of this question which we ought to separate in our minds. One is the plan-making process and the other is the implementing process.

In Britain the regional plans have been initiated by and become the responsibility of the central government. They have been done in consultation with the local authorities and other interests. Experience in projects such as the South-East Study has convinced us that much of what is important to a regional study is national: the initial assumptions you make about the region's place in the national economy are the beginning of the process, and national considerations are important in the final phase when you are considering how much public capital you are going to invest, where it is coming from and how it fits into the whole system of national priorities. It is difficult to see any system working in this country where the government surrenders these all-important assumptions and proposals to any other agency. Any other kind of body attempting this could not see the national picture and could not be so close to government thinking and policy as to make sense of its region in national terms.

Regional plans in Britain, which hitherto have dealt primarily with land use, will come increasingly into the economic sphere and will become (depending on the kind of government we have) very much more concerned with industry and the effect of regional proposals on the industrial structure of the region. Here again only the central government will be able to handle the material that will make up the industrial-economic parts of the plan.

If it was necessary or right to have a regionally elected local authority to make the plan, we should have to invent a completely new type of local government system to do it, superimposed on the existing structure. It would take a long time to alter the existing structure in such a radical way and it would take quite a long time for this new machinery to settle down. Meanwhile we have got to get on and make some regional plans against the background of an articulated national plan. Because of the kinds of assumption and decision that have to be made and the time factor, and because I do not think the government can surrender this responsibility to anyone else, in the end this function must be primarily the responsibility of central government.

Having said that, I want to say that not only do the present regional plans have many defects, but the procedures are defective. I should like to see the next round of regional plans done more comprehensively and in much closer consultation with a whole range of interests—the local authorities, industry, labour, the universities and so on. This is a difficult thing to do. Whereas in the smaller regions, such as the North-East, it is a perfectly feasible operation, in the South-East and the North-West it is in practical manpower terms a very large commitment. Consultation with local interests should involve them at the very beginning of the planning operation. The South-East Study, being a published series of proposals for discussion, may conceivably point the way to a valuable procedure for the future.

I turn briefly to the question of implementation. Having made your regional plan, related it to the national economy, and decided how much money you will spend on it, you must then implement it and put it on the ground. At that stage three agencies come into operation—the central government, the local authorities and the new town corporations (perhaps on a regional basis and handling also town expansion). I therefore see implementation as primarily a responsibility for central government working very closely in partnership with the local authorities and all the other people concerned with the special building programmes that require concentrated effort and investment —a process which might be controlled by a regional adaptation of the new town corporation.

A lively discussion ensued among the British members. It was sparked off by Professor Self, who ventured to summarise the differences of approach expressed by Mr Cohen and Mr Jones in these terms: in America the general approach is to allow each city to expand and grow by itself; in Britain the planner regards this approach as chaos and wants to decide everything from the centre.

Dame Evelyn Sharp said the central government was not trying to dictate regional plans: it was merely trying to offer a strategy for the different regions and to indicate what help it could give. Someone had to start this process; then the proposals were discussed with the local authorities and the regions would take their different shapes, which was what Professor Self had been asking for.

Mr Wells thought the tragedy of the South-East Study was that it had been published at the same time as a government statement accepting its proposals. Thus, in the minds of the people who were always suspicious of Whitehall, it appeared to be a *diktat*. He much preferred the system, used at the time of the Beveridge Report, whereby a scheme was produced and published before the government said whether they liked it or not.

Mr Jones replied that the South-East Study was a framework for action. The government identified the major strategies, but they were bound to leave a wide range of choice to the local authorities as to how they should handle a lot of the growth and plan a lot of the smaller projects. For example, if Kettering was to be a new town, there was no reason why the local authority should not give the central government their ideas for handling growth in that part of the country. The Study was not a *diktat*, but a backcloth against which other people had got to do something. He added: 'Unless we indicate the facts, the trends, the assumptions and the government's willingness to take certain steps—and primarily, of course, to spend money—then nobody can make a move. That is why we did the South-East Study: no one in the South-East could make a move until we did it.'

Mr James: In 1947 the Government said that it would give the local planning authorities guidance as to what was the population target on which they should base their plans. How was I, as a professional officer, to discharge this responsibility towards the Home Counties if we had to continue acting on the quite inadequate guide given by the Abercrombie Plan? Where was the responsibility to give leadership in this direction, so that local planning authorities could get on with their job? Immediately a sign of leadership is given on a responsibility that was laid down in 1947, you jib. This seems fantastic.

Professor Self: I recognise the case for central decision in these matters but I am also a little alarmed at the way in which central decisions can cramp local initiative. I want a relationship which will combine a central framework and a degree of central initiative with a degree of local initiative and local energy. We have not found the right formula for this yet.

Mr Jones: In order to get that partnership of central leadership and local initiative, which I entirely accept, I do not think it is necessary to invent a new and different kind of local authority.

Mr Tankel: What is the next step in the South-East?

Mr Jones: We are now finishing consultations with the bodies concerned, including the NEDC and the planning authorities. At the end of the year, depending on the Government, we intend to review the whole thing in the light of what people have said and then it will be for the Government of the day to decide whether to go on with it in its present form, to change it or to relate it differently to the rest of the country, and to decide how much to spend on a building and investment programme for the next five to ten years.

Mr Tankel: But is the South-East Study a plan at the moment, or is there another step which should be taken at the regional scale?

Mr Jones: The Study contains proposals for major growth and major projects and also target populations which the local authorities must put into their own development plans.

Mr Senior thought this was the crucial point: how was the South-East Study's regional strategy to be translated into a regional plan? He was fully in agreement with Mr Jones that regional strategy-making was essentially a central government function; if there was any question of deciding between development at, for example, Kettering or Peterborough, then the central government should decide. No one had suggested that this sort of decision should be delegated to an elected regional authority; what should be the function of a representative regional authority was the making of a development plan within the framework of the strategy thus laid down by central government. It was for this purpose that he had suggested that authorities elected on a city-regional basis should be substituted for the existing top-tier local authorities, which had shown themselves incapable of discharging their development-planning functions in the metropolitan regions.

Mr Jones had admitted that the Greater London Council ought to have been given a wider area, but had claimed that even so it was a big advance. 'Of course it was a big advance,' Mr Senior went on. 'It brought us in one five-year stride from where London local government was in 1889 to where it ought to have been in 1939. If we can make the next fifty-year stride in five years we could be up to date three years from now. But Mr Jones is suggesting that we should let it lie for another generation or so. That is what I object to.'

Mr Jones had said that the Greater London Council would be able to examine the main planning problems of London as a whole. So it would: but it would not be able to do anything about them if the neighbouring counties would not co-operate. 'You are saying', Mr Senior continued, 'that the next stage is to make development plans, which you are going to leave to the local authorities. I was at a public enquiry last week where the Kent County Council made it very clear that they were not going to alter their 1953 development plan, based on the Abercrombie assumption of no further increase in the population of the London region.' If the government did not supersede the plan-making authorities in the London metropolitan region with an elective regional authority it would have to do the plan-making job itself—and that, Mr Senior argued, would be utterly inconsistent with the whole basis of local government in Britain. He also suggested that to describe it as unrealistic to propose so extensive a reorganisation of local government just did not make sense when one compared what the British government was up against with what Mr Cohen had described New York as being up against. Ten years before, even the Lancashire County Council had been willing to accept regional authorities for Merseyside and the Manchester city region, because at that time it had been possible for the Local Government Commission to recommend a continuous county for mid-Lancashire also. The only reason why the county council were against continuous counties now was that the present Local Government Commission could not do this. Mr Jones was asking us to accept pure defeatism for no other reason than that we had just made a very big advance.

Sir William Hart agreed with Mr Senior about the function of the South-East Study. It was a most valuable thing from the point of view of getting everybody to face the facts of life. And it really was the facts of life that were bothering the South-East area. He also agreed with Mr Wells that because the Study came out coupled with a White Paper, it had looked very much like a plan. Having got this far we must now face the second process of making the plan. He did not subscribe to the view that we had to have an entirely new form of local authority: this would take much time and cause many problems. The Greater London Council, which would also take some time to get started, had not a sufficiently wide area if we were really talking about regional planning: at present it could only undertake urban planning. If the areas outside the green belt were not willing to co-operate in a way which made possible a unified approach to the problems, we might still get the same sort of result as the South-East Study had proposed, but its execution would meet resistances and it would not be done in the best way. The problem was how to get a unified approach. He did not believe that the central government could satisfactorily execute a regional plan.

One thing which had been done in the London area over the last few years was to get together a group of local planning authorities, roughly speaking from the commuter range. This Standing Conference on London Regional Planning had not been going very long; it was a very tender plant. Its object was not to produce uniformity but to try to do at a lower level what the South-East Study was doing—to start people thinking. It was at any rate a mechanism which, if it could keep alive and did not run into too many fundamental difficulties, could accomplish the second stage—getting the local authorities to think alike. He did not say they would agree—they probably would not—but at least they would have a common understanding. This was not a bad start if it could be kept going; it might be a partial solution to the problems confronting New York, though of course these were on a vastly bigger scale.

Mr Cohen endorsed Mr Senior's view of the relative amounts of political courage required to deal with the situation in the New York region and in Britain. In the last few months a major effort by the four chief executives in the New York metropolitan area (three governors and the Mayor) to set up, with Federal support, a tri-state transportation planning committee had been vetoed by the refusal of one state legislature to pass enabling legislation. 'I am not sure what else we can do,' he added, 'but continue to exercise ingenuity in devising new ways of building up a broad and informed consensus on these issues, winning political support for co-operative activities and answering uninformed charges.'

Mr Slayton said the United States could never claim responsibility for exercising the sort of directional authority within a region—particularly an urban region—that the British government was acknowledged to have. It could take an initiative by putting Federal resources into a region in order to improve its economy, but it did not try to guide regional growth. Any suggestion that it should do so would be bitterly resented by the states and would never be accepted by Congress or by local officials. He thought Mr Cohen's suggestion that there should be some device within central government to co-ordinate Federal grant programmes so that they could be used to assist the planned development of metropolitan regions was a good one, but it assumed the existence of regional plans and mechanisms for carrying them out, which did not in fact exist.

6

REGIONAL STUDIES

In the sixth session the different approaches to regional planning in Britain and the United States were illustrated in detail by reference to current plans for the London and Washington metropolitan regions. Mr James dealt with London and the background to the South-East Study in his preliminary paper, which read as follows:

About fifty years ago Sir Holford Mackinder was writing in *Britain and the British Seas*: 'In a manner all South-eastern England is a single urban community . . . A city in an economic sense is no longer an area covered continuously with streets and houses.' This year my department has published the South-East Study—a planning study for this urban community, which effectively treats the whole South-East as a region for the first time.

Mackinder's picture of metropolitan England, dominated by one great centre, London, with a few smaller concentrations such as Portsmouth, is still recognisable but its character has altered considerably. Since then the first drastic changes in our urban morphology have become only too apparent. London has spread radially outwards, absorbing small towns and villages. The higher housing standards adopted after 1918, the lower densities possible on cheap farmland while agriculture was at a low ebb, facilitated by the extension of bus and rail services and re-emphasised by the motor-car, gave us inter-war sprawl and an impetus to centrifugal movement from London that is still with us, while expanding employment opportunities have reinforced the centripetal attractions of the metropolis.

The first plan for the metropolis was not really a plan at all. This was the report of the Royal Commission on the Distribution of the Industrial Population (called the Barlow Report after its chairman), presented in 1940, which was the basis of twenty years' thinking for the region. Recent commentators have pointed out that it was fundamentally anti-metropolitan, as was the planning based upon it. The Commission concluded that 'the continued *drift* of the industrial population to London and the Home Counties constitutes a social, economic and strategical problem which demands instant attention'.

They advocated severe restriction of further *industrial* building to check continued physical growth, and a progressive reshaping of London itself by redevelopment and the dispersal of industry and population to cure the evils of overcrowding in the inner areas. The importance of this stage in the development of our thinking was that it linked town-planning policies, previously too much a matter of layout, with wider policies for the distribution of industry and population. If some of its assumptions were wrong—e.g., that drift was the population problem and manufacturing industry the key to controlling employment growth—it nevertheless provided a clear directive, a basis both for the plans and for action while the plans were being made. Without it our present problems would be even more difficult. A measure of the success of the distribution policies based on the Barlow Report is that for every five people who left Wales in the 1920s and for every three who left Cumberland, Durham and Northumberland, only one left in the 1950s.

The next stage in the planning of the London region was the series of great advisory plans—the County of London Plan, 1943, the Greater London Plan, 1944, and the City of London Plan, 1947. In 1946 the government accepted the principles of the Greater London Plan, which aimed to restrain urban sprawl, to provide better living conditions, especially in the inner areas, to reduce journeys to work by redistributing population and employment, to relieve traffic congestion and to improve communications. Its two most important assumptions were that no new industry would be allowed, except in very special cases, and that the population of the region as a whole would not rise above the 1938 level. (This was in line with national population forecasts, which expected a levelling-off of population.) The Greater London Plan envisaged redevelopment of Inner London for a population one and a quarter millions below the 1938 level. It expected the suburban population to remain stable. Around the built-up area of London it advised the establishment of a green belt, five miles wide, to be maintained as open land—except that 300,000 Londoners were to be housed there, partly in out-county estates to be built by the London County Council and partly by infilling and the limited, compact expansion of existing settlements. Beyond the green belt half a million Londoners were to be housed in new towns and 400,000 by the expansion of existing towns. Industry and commerce were to move with population in an operation closely linked with redevelopment.

The Greater London Plan had at least one penetrating critic in the 1940s. Professor Wooldridge said that it exhibited 'the incurable defects of planning working outwards from a metropolitan centre'. He thought the area it covered was too small and forecast that the strength of London's attractions would only overflow into the rest of the South-East if restrictive policies were applied to too small an area.

In 1956 my department reviewed the progress of Greater London planning in its annual report. The population of the region had grown, but this was mainly due to natural increase; although there was considerable inward and outward flow there was no evidence of a net gain due to migration and it was considered that there were as yet no grounds for changing the population assumptions of the plan. Dispersal policies were beginning to show results in population and industrial employment trends, but overall employment growth in the London region had been 9 per cent between 1948 and 1955, compared with 6 per cent in England and Wales; the region was increasing its share of national employment. Services and administration had shown the greatest growth and the advantages of decentralising office employment were recognised for the first time.

The disquieting nature of the trends first noticed in that official review became increasingly evident during the next two or three years. The birth-rate had begun to climb markedly in 1955, and continued to do so. (It has still not slackened.) Employment in Central London was expanding rapidly. Traffic congestion was becoming more and more intolerable. The green belt was undergoing pressure for the housing of Londoners. A close re-examination of the assumptions and aims of the Greater London Plan culminated temporarily in the South-East Study and the Government White Paper: temporarily a) because the Study and White Paper are not plans—a period of negotiation must follow—and b) because the trends must be kept under constant review, for it is clear that it is the assumptions more than the principles of the Greater London Plan that have been falsified by events.

The South-East Study expects three and a half million more people in the South-East region by 1981. This has been accepted by the government as a basis for planning. It is a very modest figure. The largest single element in this growth is expected to be natural increase. A net migration gain of 1.1 million people is expected. Part of this will be movement south on retirement. Greater economic prosperity in other parts of the country is unlikely to affect this movement, but the Study does assume that serious efforts will continue to be made to provide more jobs in the North, in Scotland and in Wales. The assumed migration rate is less than the projection of current trends.

The pattern which emerges from these proposals is interesting because it is so old. The increasing relative concentration of activity in the South-East is a reversion to the pre-Industrial-Revolution pattern. The South-East Study proposals are similarly a strengthening of those elements in the existing settlement pattern of the South-East which are best able to counteract the steadily expanding dominance of London. The aims have changed, the location factors have changed, the circumstances may appear to have changed out of all recognition, but the proposed pattern of major expansions is completely recognisable. We are proposing to strengthen the London-Bristol axis (Bristol was formerly our second largest port) and the London-Portsmouth axis, which in fact converge on London Airport. We are recognising in Bletchley, Banbury, and Northampton the economic strength of the London-Midland axis. We

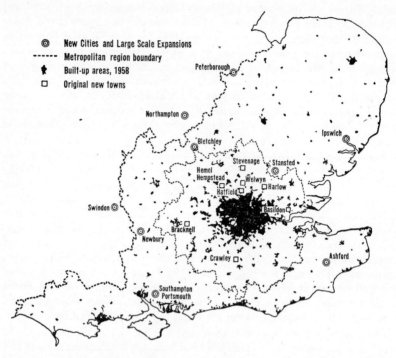

South-East England: Major development proposals

are strengthening the old axis flung out from London into the continental angle—into Essex and into Kent; and with Peterborough, Northampton, Banbury, Swindon and Bedford we are re-emphasising the importance in the settlement pattern of South-East England of the scarpland-vale structure. There is really only one new element in the whole pattern and that is the proposed development of Stansted as a new town and a new airport.

Enlarging on his paper, Mr James began by emphasising that in Britain it was the Minister who was responsible to Parliament for planning, and it was the Minister who approved, with or without modifications, the development plans put up by the local authorities as agents responsible to him; therefore the Minister had a direct responsibility for all that happened in terms of land use throughout the country. In preparing their first development plans the local authorities had proceeded on the assumption that the government's adoption of the

Barlow policy for industrial location relieved them of any obligation to plan for more than their own natural increase in population, which was expected to decline after the immediate post-war rise. The government had specifically approved the Abercrombie regional plan for Greater London, which embodied these assumptions, as the basis for development planning in the Home Counties. But by 1955 the population had begun to rise again—and thereafter continued to climb—while service employment was seen to be increasingly pulled into the London area, where three-quarters (by rateable value) of Britain's offices were located. Meanwhile, with increasing prosperity, London families living in overcrowded conditions were wanting to buy their own homes, young people were marrying earlier and old people were living longer and able to afford separate homes. Consequently the average household size had dropped from 3·05 to 2·85 persons between 1951 and 1961.

'All this,' Mr James went on, 'means that though there has been a tremendous effort to house the people of London, there still remains, in the immediate future and on the most modest estimates, a clear need to build at least half a million new homes for Londoners. The green belt surrounds them, and under the threat of more house-building every county around London has made proposals to deepen the green belt by adding to its originally approved 840 square miles another 1,200 square miles, which would push it out a distance of ten to twenty miles farther from the edge of Greater London. Where can the new houses go?

'This, basically, is what the whole exercise is about. This is the responsibility of the planning authorities and ourselves—to make allocations of land for housing as well as we can. Land already allocated is running out. Many of the local authorities close to London have none at all. Farther out there may be enough for another four or five years. Prices are rising as a consequence of this and the brake has to be taken off. Immediately we asked the question of how and where this should be done we had to consider for what size of future population growth we had to plan in order to give guidance to the local authorities in making their development plans. Here we had to take a national view. The answer really rested on a judgment about what was likely to happen to the economy of the country and on a recognition by us that the tools available to us might (without harm to our economy) effect marginal changes in the distribution pattern of the population, but not really fundamental changes—certainly not up to 1970.

'Nor can one say what is in fact for any region a desirable distribution of population, or what is the norm for the distribution of population in this country. The South-East is one of the most densely populated parts of Britain, but it is only London itself that is really congested; the rest is a relatively open area. So one cannot start from the base that the South-East is so overcrowded that we must even send the babies that have been born in the South-East northwards. Quite clearly one can accept the fact that for a long time a growth of population can be provided for, so long as it is done in an orderly way. If we look back in our history we find that the South-East was always the area of densest population. The page was turned for a time when the North took over during the nineteenth century, simply because the coalfields and the textile industry were there. That page has been turned back with the coming of electricity and the new processes in our industrial economy.

'Whatever way one looks at it one cannot establish for any one region an optimum population. We must look to see what the economy is likely to give us, whether the out-movement of population from the less prosperous regions is too rapid in social terms, and how far it may have to be slowed down, by pumping money and new capital into roads, schools, house-building and industry, in order to assist those areas to make the transition more slowly and more gracefully.

'So the assumption was made that we would plan for some diminution in the scale of migration to the South-East and that the target for extra population in the South-East should be three and a half millions. This is half a million less than the continuation of existing trends would yield. However, this estimate may be too small if the population continues to mount, as it looks as if it may well do, and if we are not successful in putting more industries into the North-East. If we also take into account the 1961 age structure the figure may be about four millions. So we have taken a conservative estimate. But this does not really matter when we are dealing with this kind of figure because at this stage the important thing is to find ways of coping with any really big increase.

'When first we look at London itself we see that it has been losing population over the last ten years. An outward movement has been taking place of people seeking more space and the open countryside. During these ten years the total loss to London was about 180,000, and this loss would be likely to continue under redevelopment. We simply cannot put back, into most of the slum areas the LCC is tackling, the same number of people as were there before. Land is needed for roads, better schools, space for cars, etc., and these requirements take four acres out of every nine that are redeveloped for housing. Even where we put up tall blocks of flats the population tends to decline and the private outward movement reinforces this trend. Even so, we have not said in the Study that we should plan for a further diminution of the population of London. We shall in fact make every effort to make it a higher-density area than it has been. We have said that we would like to set an aim of eight millions. London's population is at present eight millions. This means that we must offset the decline of population that is taking place. It is going to be a very difficult thing to do.

'If, then, we cannot put more people into London, the three and a half million extra people must be housed outside. We cannot touch the green belt. This means that the towns that surround the green belt must be expanded in some way. This must happen. We cannot overnight stop the growth of office employment in Central London, which has recently been rising at a rate of 20,000 a year. To do so might be terribly damaging to our economy; in any case, the chances that we could do so are very remote indeed. The commuting population is likely to continue to grow at least for some time. Whether it will continue to grow in the 1970s we just do not know. We hope not, because the conditions of travel to work are already very difficult. (Incidentally in London 90 per cent of commuters use public transport and only 10 per cent use private cars.) We must therefore try to get some of the offices in London to move out, initially to the Croydon area, then to Watford and similar towns, and by successive stages farther out still into the towns of the outer metropolitan belt, to the rest of South-East England and if possible into towns in the North and South-West.

'We took a decision that to impose this three and a half million population on the metropolitan region would be too much of a burden and we aimed to plan communities for one and a quarter million people in areas well beyond the green belt where there seemed to be the best opportunities for growth. Southampton offered good port facilities and excellent opportunities for an industrial hinterland, which had not been developed while Southampton was primarily a passenger port. As the economy changes, with London Airport taking increasing numbers of passengers, Southampton is likely to become more of a cargo port: the Rochdale Committee commented on this. On the London-Bristol road we have suggested another development in the Newbury area. Thirdly, the Bletchley-Northampton area was suggested as a site for the development of another major city. These cities would have populations of about 250,000. Looking to the Channel, with the possibility of a Channel

Tunnel, we have also suggested the development of a new town at Ashford, and another at Stansted on account of the new air terminal there. These towns would thus be related to a new communication network—motorway, rail, airport and Channel Tunnel. Other towns which already exist we should like to see enlarged.

'We have never before planned for new cities of about 250,000 and this is perhaps the most exciting thing for us to face in the future. How can this be done? What kind of services must be provided for population clusters of this magnitude? How far can they be centralised? What form is development to take—a series of beads on a necklace, a linear pattern or the radial structure that exists in many of our towns? Should the town be spread over a distance of twenty-five miles or ten miles across and broken down into segments of 60,000 to 70,000, but with a common core for various services? This is the theme on which I should like to hear of any research work that is being done in the United States which could be of help to us.'

In response to this SOS Mr Tankel offered two suggestions: first, that planning for the expansion of urban regions should concentrate on the commercial-industrial-cultural component (which should be tightly designed) and the regional-scale transportation network, leaving the remaining residential communities (perhaps 80 per cent by area) to be dealt with flexibly as they came along, based on general standards and guidelines; and secondly, for London itself, that expansion should occur within the green belt, with new sub-centres on the major radials, accompanied by vast acquisitions of public park land in the wedges between, especially in places where nature intended, such as the Chilterns, the Sussex Downs and the Thames Valley. Such a pattern would not deny London and would better serve the region than the relatively isolated new towns and the arbitrary green belt by providing more people with better access to jobs and cultural facilities and to meaningful countryside. Mr Winnick, however, regarded his emphasis on the strong city centre as unduly influenced by circumstances peculiar to New York, and Mr James said no one had disproved Buchanan's thesis that it was impossible for a fully motorised society to have all the present functions of a central area concentrated in a big city centre without getting into two levels of movement, which was very expensive. Mr Tankel disputed this: provided a new city had a large enough centre of activity to support an attractive public transportation system, so that people could get to a wide choice of facilities by public transport and were not tempted to use their cars to go to work in the centre, he argued, a motorised society could and should have centres catering for populations of anywhere between one and three million people.

Mr Bor agreed that the city must basically depend on public transport; the bigger the city, the more essential public transport became, and the more closely the shape of the city must be related to the form of public transport (perhaps the monorail) that was adopted. But he would not put all the eggs in one basket: he would like to see facilities for culture, entertainment, specialised shopping and specialised headquarter offices concentrated in a region's major centre, but he saw no reason why the ordinary offices, which attracted the bulk of the commuter traffic, should not be located in sub-centres grouped round major district centres. Against this Professor Rapkin maintained that a large and increasingly important component of the turnover of city-centre shops consisted of lunch-hour sales to office workers. He was in favour of removing industry from the city centre, but to remove offices too would be to lose the advantage of enabling one trip to serve two purposes; the result would either be to prevent the satisfaction of specialised shopping needs or to introduce another system of transportation to meet this demand elsewhere, and thus to cancel out the economic advantage of reducing commuter traffic to and from the centre. Unless we made full use of the values we created and the economies in transportation we made possible when we developed the city centre as the point of optimum accessibility from all surrounding areas, we could not enjoy the full benefits of metropolitan living.

Dr Lichfield accepted this view in principle, but thought we must ask ourselves whether there were not other functions besides industry that the city centre could dispense with to the net benefit of the people it served. There was no presumption in favour of perpetuating, in the same proportions and quantities, the accumulation of functions in our city centres that we had inherited from the past. Professor Self pointed out that, granted the advantages of having offices concentrated in large centres, it did not follow that metropolitan London should be the only commercial centre for the whole of Britain. If office employment could with advantage be dispersed from central London to large sub-centres within the London metropolitan region, why not to places like Ipswich and Southampton? And if to such places, why not to the big northern cities? Mr James replied that research into these questions was in progress.

As to the mechanism for the creation of big new cities, it was agreed that development corporations would have to be set up *ad hoc*, and that each development corporation must be free to pursue individually 'the objective of creating the most attractive place in the world for people to live in'.

Other speakers took up Mr Tankel's second theme; were the new big centres being located at the right distance from London? Mr James thought it was immaterial whether they were inside or outside London's metropolitan region, provided they were in places where they would release a geographical potential for growth; but it was politically unrealistic to consider putting them in the approved green belt, even though half of it was already used for such urban purposes as recreation. Mr May pointed out that the strategy adopted in the Study, though it met the needs of the South-East for the time being, could not meet them for all time: it might eventually be desirable to reverse the dispersal process. This was not a matter of great concern so far as the individual new-city projects went, though their pattern and target sizes might have to be changed at some time in the future. What was essential, however, was that they should be planned within an overall transportation framework. Mr Brooke Taylor thought they might well be bigger and located farther from London: but the important thing, in his view, was that they should be designed as integral parts of whatever regions they were in, and not (like the original new towns) as free-standing entities. This implied that each new city must be so related to existing communities that it could in due course be absorbed with them into a regional unit under an elected authority, and the strategy should be conceived with this ultimate objective in mind.

Professor Mandelker insisted that the green belt, for all its weaknesses, was working well and should not be invaded: neither Britain nor America had found any other way of solving the regional open-space problem and protecting tracts of undeveloped countryside. At this point Professor Wibberley protested that we all seemed to be ignoring the existence in the South-Eastern countryside of a highly developed and intricately organised settlement pattern, with country towns ten to twelve miles apart and villages thick on the ground. Three out of four of these settlements were now surplus to the needs of the rural economy, and could therefore absorb much of the increase in the urban population. But there might be very great pressure on them from people who did not want to live in big towns. Other speakers agreed that the plan for any new city must take account of its impact on neighbouring villages and the surrounding countryside—as the Livingston Plan would, but the other new town plans had not.

Dr Lichfield asked how the government's policy for the location of industry would be geared to the provision of employment in the new cities. Would industry be dispersed from London or allowed to come from all parts of the country? Would the distance between London and the new cities be conditioned by the need to preserve industrial linkages? Mr James replied that there would be no free entry: the South-East would have to take second place to the growth points established in other parts of the country. Hence the need to locate the new cities where they might not only attract employment from London but also generate local industries.

Asked whether he would plan to accommodate another three and a half million people in the South-East if there were no economic or political difficulties in the way of moving industry and population about the country, he said he would dearly like to reduce the size of London and the employment at its centre, but we had to be realistic. Mr Senior suggested that this population increase should rather be regarded as a positive opportunity to create new regional centres in the South-East. The trouble with the South-East was that it had only one regional centre, which must also serve as the national capital; but given half a dozen big new centres all its people could have ready access to regional services and facilities.

Mr Harris wound up this discussion with a list of questions on which research should be undertaken.

a) What was the configuration and minimum size of a city that would support rail transport?
b) Did rail transport offer any advantages over motorised mass transportation?
c) Was there an irreconcilable conflict between mass transport and car transport in a city centre serving more than 200,000 people?
d) How could a city centre be planned so flexibly that it could grow from 250,000 to a million?
e) How could the new cities in the South-East be brought within half an hour's travel of the centre of London?
f) Could such cities be put on the London telephone exchange?
g) Were there in London complexes of office activity that could be moved bodily to a single new centre?

All these questions, Mr Harris added, must be put in the context of the fact that London was the real growth magnet of the South-East.

Mr Gutheim then gave an account of the Washington Year 2000 Plan. He said:

The City of Washington has several distinctive features. It is, of course, the national capital and it is also the fastest growing metropolitan area in the United States. This is not generally appreciated; people tend to think of its monumental and relatively unchanging centre but neglect the booming suburbs. Its central city, the District of Columbia, which is the traditional constitutional city and seat of government, did in fact lose population during the census period of 1940 to 1960. Washington is also in the southern and most rapidly growing sector of the east coast urban belt, which the geographer Jean Gottman has named 'Megalopolis'. Much of its present growth appears to be due to its relationship with this urban belt and the development of non-Federal functions, rather than to its earlier sources of growth as an administrative capital.

Washington is a formal city. Together with the smaller and earlier nearby colonial capitals of Williamsburg and Annapolis, it is the only example of a baroque city plan that we have. This plan, laid out in 1790, is still preserved to a remarkable degree in its characteristic patterns of radials, circles and other baroque features, whose preservation is a mandatory consideration. As one attempts to deal with any of the characteristic problems of this area, these relatively fixed features become very important.

Washington has had 164 years of planning of a greater or lesser intensity, with periods of great activity and periods of great neglect. The period 1945–50 was one of stultification: there was obsolete planning machinery and no way of dealing with the problems of regional growth, while the problems of rapid change in the central city were generally ignored. In 1950 the Federal Government decided that, to strengthen the national security and offer some protection against nuclear attack, the continuity of the Federal Government should be ensured by the dispersal of public offices. This meant specifically, in the case of Washington, that no new Federal buildings were to be erected within a radius of twenty miles from the zero target area. The result was the decentralisation of such establishments as the Atomic Energy Commission, the Bureau of Standards, the Central Intelligence Agency and the National Security Agency. Today, partly as the result of this policy and partly as the result of earlier moves such as those of the National Health Centre and the Space Laboratory, some two-thirds of the Federal employees in the Washington area live outside the District of Columbia and one-third work outside.

A major consequence of this dispersal was to remove the growth of the Federal establishment from the jurisdiction of the city's planning agency. A second consequence was that, with no plan for the dispersal of these Federal offices, it was very difficult for the four counties around Washington to make their own plans. These counties were very much aware of their own insignificance when attempting to deal with the Federal Government.

The result of this position was the creation in 1950 of a Regional Planning Commission, of which I was chairman. The first thing this commission did was to press for a reform of the planning machinery. In 1952 we were able to secure an enactment by Congress which created for the central city (the Federal District) the National Capital Planning Commission (NCPC) and for the peripheral county area the National Capital Regional Planning Council (NCRPC). The Regional Planning Commission had ultimate responsibility for all Federal questions in the area, but only after formal consultation with the NCPC and the NCRPC, on which the surrounding local authorities are represented.

The next major development was the creation of a circumferential highway, which is now completed, and to this are connected a series of radial highways. The effect of these sixty-mile-an-hour highways and of the dispersal of the Federal agencies has been an intensive highway orientation. The consequences of this soon became apparent. None of the locations chosen for Federal agencies recognised the need to organise the journey to work in such large employment centres in terms of mass transportation rather than the private automobile. Thus the highways have become major arteries for commuter traffic within the region and are equipped with the necessary interchanges throughout their length.

The crux of the transportation problem is the peak-hour movement of traffic in the early morning and late afternoon. If you construct your highways in order to cope with peak-hour travel you have an enormous bill. A more efficient way must be found of moving peak-hour traffic. A recent study of transport in Washington showed that the worst areas of traffic congestion are not in the downtown area but in the suburbs. The reaction to this was to authorise the NCRPC to make a study of the mass-transport situation in the Washington area. The report of this study in 1959 proposed the creation of a rapid rail transport system that should be integrated with the highway plan. In the centre of Washington, where consideration for the amenities of the city had never allowed overhead wires for a street-car system, it was proposed to put the mass-transport system in subways.

The Year 2000 Plan was commenced almost concurrently with the beginning of the mass-transport survey and reflected the direction of an energetic and imaginative Californian, who thought it proper that we should not only respond to this tremendous growth and change but should also put to the Washington community as positively and dramatically as possible the serious alternatives which they then faced. It was felt at that time that an immediate response was necessary to meet the problems of outward urban sprawl and of the creation of a suitable transport system. This background has an important bearing on the spirit in which the Plan was undertaken and the type of planning strategy that was adopted.

The outline of the Plan is very simple. It begins with some remarks about the city as it stands—its history, present characteristics and the values which should be preserved—and then comes immediately to the heart of the problem, i.e., the rapid growth that is now taking place. It deals with the sources of this growth and projects it for periods of twenty and forty years. It analyses it in terms of employment, income and other significant characteristics, and interprets these in terms of what can be done to accommodate this growth. It gives a concise view of the objectives and goals that should be aimed at. It states what it rejects. It goes on to recommend the creation of relatively compact, well-planned suburban communities; the concentration of these communities in corridors radiating from the centre of the city; greater reliance on mass transportation; limitation of the freeway system largely to the routes already planned; urban employment to be concentrated in the centre with the exception that two-thirds of Federal employment should be located elsewhere in the region; urban renewal of most of the original city; no increase of population within the District of Columbia (which now has about 800,000 people); and the preservation of greater portions of the countryside as open space (some 300,000 acres within the region). There can be no doubt what these words mean but their meaning was reinforced by a simple diagrammatic statement of what this city should be.

The Plan then began to deal with the question of implementing this concept of a radial-corridor metropolitan area. How do you actually build the separate communities and these corridors along which they are to be strung? At that point it ran into a lack of planning powers and development initiative. It had to be recognised, first, that the planners were way out on the frontier of the American political and legal system, and secondly that there was no way by which these deficiencies in law and administration could be defined in order that the right response could be obtained.

There have been very great demographic changes in the centre of the city of Washington. 84 per cent of the students in the school system of the District of Columbia are Negroes. 63 per cent of the population in the area is Negro— and this despite the fact that the Negro proportion of 20 per cent of the two million population of the entire metropolitan area has not changed by 1 per cent since the emancipation of the slaves in 1863. In other words we are dealing with a great concentration of all the Negro population in the old, sub-standard, low-income housing areas of Washington. This must be realised if the essential nature of the centre of the city is to be understood: it is not just a vacuum or a shopping centre but is inhabited by a different kind of people. The Year 2000 Plan recognises this.

The deliberate intention had been to excite people, to stimulate them, to generate a certain response and to allow this reaction to strengthen planning

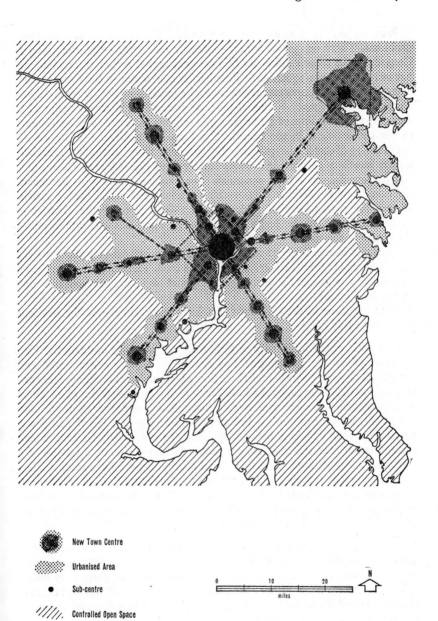

New Town Centre

Urbanised Area

Sub-centre

Controlled Open Space

Main Communication Lines

0   10   20
miles

N

The Radial Corridor Plan for the Washington Region, 2000.

institutions and to increase the capability of the area to deal with these problems. There was an extremely important side-effect—the awakening of Congress to its responsibility for this national capital region as a region, and not only for the ten-square-mile jurisdiction mentioned in the Constitution. There was also an important response in the creation of the National Capital Transportation Agency, a special-purpose authority which was designed to deal with the main lines of suburban rapid rail transport and to give assistance to the development in the centre. The Plan had a direct bearing on the appreciation of certain things which the joint committee has studied, especially on the measures to provide a water supply from the Potomac River which was protected from sewage pollution. The Plan also caused an immediate reaction from the White House: the President has established a special adviser for national-capital regional affairs—not just for the District of Columbia. The Plan also had a direct effect on many of the efforts to replan the centre of the city.

Thus this planning report was highly successful in a country where we say that documents of this kind are written to be filed. This document has shown remarkable vitality and has generated a response from, and provided direction to, public thinking.

What are some of the criticisms that have been raised over the last four years about this Plan?

a) One critic at the University of California attempted to evaluate the Plan in terms of its assumption that this should be a more concentrated and structured city and that the radial corridors were a desirable thing. His conclusion was that Washington had too many of the characteristics of an ultra-modern metropolitan area to allow this, because of the need of the people who live in this area for multiplied linkages with one another. His thinking was based on studies which he had earlier made of the Los Angeles area, where the automobile and the freeways are simply the expression of the desire of a tremendous population to have this sort of relationship with one another: they are changing jobs rapidly and are in jobs where different kinds of relationship of an often unpredictable kind are appearing. This is the sort of thing which, in this critic's opinion, is so contradictory to the tidy, neat, structured pattern of concentration within a regional city.

b) Another critic went immediately to the clause in the Plan which advocated large regional cities and said something with which I find myself in agreement: we need cities of from 250,000 to 400,000 population, the purpose of which will be to receive large, rather characteristic pieces of Washington. He criticised the corridor conception as composed primarily of smaller-scale communities of the 25,000 to 50,000 range.

c) In this group of critics there are also people who argue for greater definition of the importance of the circumferential highway and its intersections with the radials, as this was expressed in what has been described as a 'drift' rather than a 'radial' type of city.

d) A group of critics was also concerned with the problem of race within the metropolitan area. This group pointed out that one section of the central district of the Washington region would be almost completely Negro and that the corridors radiating from this area would be segregated corridors of Negro employment and housing, which would perpetuate a worse pattern of segregation than anything we have today, while the remaining area would be predominantly white. This was a conception that had absolutely no recognition at all in the Year 2000 Plan.

e) Yet another critic pointed out that by encouraging the building of radial corridors you encouraged encroachment on the open space contained between the radials. This last point refers to the recommendations which suggested the preservation of 300,000 acres in the wedges between the radials. These wedges would be zoned for agricultural uses and publicly owned parkland. The development rights over this land would be purchased and positively secured by the public authority. This was not only an unprecedented dimension of open-space acquisition and preservation but was also an invocation of powers which we do not yet have. The Plan was also based on some profound misconceptions, many of which were formulated in *Megalopolis*, particularly the chapters on agriculture. In the entire area included in these wedges there is not a single farm that could pay simple interest on its investment, on the basis of any agricultural product. All this land is held at speculative prices for development purposes and the only agriculture which exists there at present is that which produces from less and less space—greenhouse horticulture, broiler factories, high-intensity dairying with imported livestock. Therefore the expectation that most of these 300,000 acres of land will be demanded by agriculture is extremely unrealistic. The problem is to provide a more realistic basis for these specifications.

Obviously it is the structural effect of the corridors that we want and not the preservation of the open space. The open space can be justified only as you need it for the largest type of conservation efforts—e.g., the abatement of air pollution or stream-valley conservation—or as you need it for a higher standard of an urban region in terms of more parks, parks for a greater variety of purposes, pathways instead of expressways. This variety of uses of open space is exercising our minds considerably at present and we are having certain difficulties to face in this direction.

The National Capital Transportation Agency, which has been designing in more detailed engineering terms the mass-transportation system of the area, also started off very bravely but was told by Congress to revise its plans because they were not fit to be acted upon. Now that the national mass-transport legislation has gone through, I think the transport plans for Washington should get some authorisation. Congress, however, is apprehensive of enterprises of this kind and wants to be assured of the costs involved and value to be gained. Nevertheless I think a start will be made even though the planning will be short-range in nature.

It is expected that the suburban authorities will be active in using their powers to prepare for the Plan and provide for open-space legislation. Three suburban counties have prepared planning reports since the Year 2000 Plan was produced, and while none of them has adhered to it they have produced some interesting ideas of their own. These have reflected particularly one feature of the metropolitan form. In Fairfax County, for example, an open-space equal to that in the Year 2000 Plan has been embraced into the county's plan, though it takes a somewhat different form. The counties have also been active in types of local legislation: e.g., the provision of comprehensive community powers under which projects like Mr Simon's Reston new town have been developed. This could not have been done had it not been for the framework and initiative which the Plan produced.

The point that needs to be stressed is that we are trying to do a tremendous amount in a very short period of time. When Mr Simon began his enterprise he looked at the Year 2000 Plan and thought it was a plan. He then looked at the Presidential directive that said the Federal Government should co-operate in the realising of this Plan and thought this meant that some Federal agencies would contribute time, resources and support to its implementation. Unfortunately none of these things has happened yet. Whether they do happen is going to depend on many uncertainties which still remain— uncertainties which Mr Simon and other people may be able to influence—but the realisation will by no means be automatic.

The Year 2000 Plan has been subject to tests and analyses, but I should stress that the Plan came first and not the analyses. If you are not doing something there is not much point in studying it. Many critics have a tendency to come up with suggestions that are not very realistic. As the Earl of Rochester put it: 'Where action ceases, thought's impertinent.'

In reply to questions Mr Gutheim explained that the NCPC had administrative planning functions in respect of highways, schools and the like, whereas the NCRPC was an advisory body reflecting the interests of local authorities in suburban areas whose planning was affected by Federal programmes. Both were financed by the Federal Government, though the regional body received some contributions from the local authorities. He expected development in the region to follow a distorted version of the Year 2000 Plan, with stronger corridors running southwards and towards Baltimore and less compact satellite communities to the north-west with populations of up to a quarter of a million. An extension of the District of Columbia to cover the developed area of the metropolis was not out of the question, given the co-operation of the states concerned, though less formal arrangements between Federal, state and local authorities were more likely than the establishment of large self-governing units; but the major present problems were in the wider fields of economic development, of regional linkage and of the relationship between urban growth and national resources.

He emphasised that the Year 2000 Plan was a set of proposals rather than a plan proper: it would be followed a year hence by a plan designed to be implemented.[1] The purpose of the Year 2000 Plan was to influence the programmes of the people concerned with water supply, sewerage, mass transportation, highways, airports, housing and community development, who were not now planning ahead. The Federal Government, which now had a large share in these programmes, needed a regional plan to pull them together; but no existing Federal department could make such a plan. The fact that the Year 2000 Plan did not have the force of law would not prevent it from being an increasingly powerful instrument for this purpose. It had Presidential endorsement, and a Federal employee was working full-time to see that all the responsible agencies paid attention to its proposals.

Mr Slayton, however, thought Mr Gutheim was over-estimating the Plan's effectiveness. It did not, he thought, have the same sort of status, or the same chance of being carried out, as the South-East Study. The Federal Government could exercise great influence in particular fields: for example it refused to subsidise the acquisition of open space unless there was an open-space programme of regional scope. But the implementation of the Plan depended on its approval by the individual local authorities. The legislation for a mass-transport system had followed the Plan, but the lines would stop short at the boundaries of the District of Columbia. Some sort of agreement on the broad lines of development might follow from the formation of another regional body, consisting of elected officials, and certainly the Year 2000 Plan had done a tremendous amount to get people in the Washington area to think about their regional problems; but there was no governmental agency that could control the location of the major functions so as to create the urban form the Plan proposed.

From the British side it was pointed out that all this was equally

---

[1] Since published as *1965–1985 Proposed Physical Development Policies for Washington, D.C.*, National Capital Planning Commission, September, 1965, Superintendent of Documents: $1.00

true of the South-East Study. Britain had two vital advantages in the public control of private development and in the central government's power to build new towns; on the other hand, in Britain the financial help given by central government to local authorities did not bear directly on the planning of open space and public transportation. Otherwise the implementation of a regional plan was as chancy a business in South-East England as in the Washington region: both lacked any form of executive regional authority, and in both regions positive planning by the central government could be frustrated by intractable local authorities.

To some of the British members it seemed that the most useful lesson they could learn from their American colleagues' experience of their common plight was the value of putting up alternative strategies for discussion at the preliminary stage. By this means, it appeared, the public and the agencies on whose goodwill and initiative the realisation of a regional plan must depend could be induced to think in regional terms, to involve themselves in the planning process and to take an intelligent—perhaps an enthusiastic—interest in the implementation of whatever strategy was eventually adopted. Much could thus be achieved in spite of major defects in administrative organisation and machinery, whereas if the central government presented only one strategy, however tentative, it inevitably provoked a negative reaction from the local authorities concerned and failed to mobilise any support from the general public, whose sympathies (if engaged at all) were apt to be with the local rebels against 'dictation from Whitehall'. But the British civil servants present did not see it that way: they thought it would be difficult to get anything achieved in a reasonable time unless the debate was concentrated on one main approach.

IMPLEMENTATION: URBAN RENEWAL

The seminar next considered a number of specific major projects, now in process of being planned and executed in American and British urban regions, as illustrations of the ways in which the two countries' approaches to regional planning worked out in practice.

The first paper of this session was given by Mr Slayton. It read (in part) as follows:

Too often in meetings of this character, we discuss our ideas on the physical and social configuration of the urban region without adequate reference to the limitations of the existing governmental and ideological framework and with inadequate thought to the mechanisms required to achieve our objectives. And frequently we fall into the trap of the single solution, arguing for a particular development pattern when in fact a variety of solutions has considerable advantage. Consumers' choice and the testing of models through experience are factors that should not be overlooked as we try to shape and organise the urban region. There is, however, one basic dichotomy among us as to our objective in the shaping of the urban region. This dichotomy, to overstate it, is between the urban concentrationist and the low-density dispersionist views. It does not go to the question of the new town or even to a discussion of densities as such in the central city; rather it goes to the basic question of whether one should continue to have the central city.

There is a school of thought that writes off the city as we have known it and proposes—to indulge in a bit of hyperbole—a pattern of dispersion with commercial concentration at cloverleaves. The argument, in my opinion, goes to the very substance of urban society. The greatness of civilisation is based on face-to-face communication and exchange. And such exchange among the leaders of society can take place only in an arena where they regularly congregate. When I think of the junior executives of a dispersed company having lunch together day after day in a beautiful campus-like environment far from the central city, I cannot help but shudder at the horror stories of inbreeding taught to me in my high-school biology class. For such intellectual inbreeding is the death-knell of a vigorous, intellectual society. The reinforcement of beliefs, the lack of exposure to different ideas can become the opium that lulls a complacent business bureaucracy into unresponsive behaviour. We should never give up the city as a market-place of ideas and ideological exposure—even though this may be limited to meeting people in different fields or merely being exposed to other members of society.

With that off my chest, let us take a look at the experience in the United States with large-scale projects to see how effective they have been in achieving certain objectives.

Our experience of governmentally-directed projects in the States has been primarily in the field of urban renewal. Previous experience stemmed from the 'green-belt towns' of the 1930s and the 'new towns' created by the Atomic Energy Commission during and after the war. These experiments are not comparable to the new-town approach of Great Britain, for in fact they were but bedroom (dormitory) communities; the government substituted itself for the private entrepreneur. In the 'green-belt towns' the demonstration was basically anti-city, an expression of low-density, almost bucolic existence for those working in the city. These 'green-belt towns' were not designed to provide employment as well as residences. They were in essence a new form of sub-division (housing estate) development.

We have also had experience of the erection by local governments, with Federal financing, of housing developments for the poor. Some of these developments cover a large area within the city; but for the most part they have been basically individual buildings or clusters of buildings and not of the scale of a large development project.

There has not been great sophistication among cities in the United States in regard to the use of urban renewal as a means of achieving public policy objectives, although in the past few years there has been an increasing awareness of its possibilities. By and large, the objective has been rather direct and simple: namely, the clearance of existing slums and the rebuilding of these areas for uses for which there was a market. In the process, another important objective has been achieved—an increase in the tax base (rateable value) of the city: the new buildings have returned more in taxes than did the slum areas. Although this is a simple and direct objective, it is rather important to most cities, for they find their tax base declining at a time when there is increasing demand for services.

Second, one should review the planning context of most of the urban-renewal projects that have been built recently and which, therefore, were planned a good many years ago. In the United States, we have relied heavily on the zoning ordinance as the means by which the city controlled or influenced development. Thus we have built up acceptance and experience with zoning-type controls—controls based upon mathematical determinations as to coverage, density, setbacks, floor-area ratios and the like. These controls were developed to apply to plots of varying sizes and shapes and thus can be applied universally, without discrimination. Hardship cases are handled through variances granted by special boards.

With this as the experience in development control, it was only natural for cities to apply similar controls to developments in urban-renewal projects. After the land had been acquired, and the new street pattern established, parcels were created and zoning-type controls applied to these parcels. Thus construction in urban-renewal areas generally took place in the same manner as did construction in non-urban-renewal areas. The result was not always a happy one; for, as we all know, zoning controls do not in and of themselves create a good design.

But more recently there has been recognition that it is possible for the local government, the city, to exercise a different kind of control and to influence the development and design of an urban-renewal area to a much greater extent and in a much more positive way. I feel we are making considerable headway through using the urban-renewal process to achieve more sophisticated objectives. At present these objectives are generally design-oriented rather than socially-oriented, but of late there has been an increasing awareness of the importance of using the renewal plan to achieve social objectives.

Here I should like to throw in a caveat. The rebuilding in urban-renewal areas, except for public housing and public buildings, must be done through the entrepreneurial process. Private developers must be interested in building what is planned and thus there must be an economic market for the proposed uses. The plan must be economically feasible. Subject to this it is a fact—often not perceived by the policy-makers and decision-makers—that in urban-renewal areas the city can determine precisely what it wants built, where it wants it built, and how it is to be built. Under urban renewal the land has been assembled by the city and its sale or lease can carry with it a precise obligation to build what the city wants built. This gives the city an enormously powerful planning tool—except for public construction, the only positive developmental tool available. Unfortunately, some local government officials have been prone to look upon the operation as a real-estate transaction only. Their interest has been in selling land at the highest possible price to the developer most willing to develop it. This process is not conducive to the achievement of much broader design and social objectives.

Let me briefly review, then, some of the experiences we have had in the States, and, without necessarily advocating any one as the best, draw some conclusions as to what elements seem important in the development of urban-renewal projects.

Charles Centre in Baltimore, Maryland, is a large, intensive downtown (central-area) project that is well along the road to success. The concept of rebuilding a major portion of downtown Baltimore stemmed from advocacy by a group of civic-minded businessmen. The purpose was to reinvigorate a downtown area that was decaying physically and economically. The concept of major surgery and major rebuilding was adopted by the city itself as a major policy but with considerable reliance upon the leadership of the civic organisations created by the businessmen to give positive direction to the planning and execution of the project. This organisation subsequently became allied with the public agencies designated to undertake the project.

The principle adopted was the creation of a very detailed plan. The project was very complicated in that it involved underground parking to be undertaken by the public, with private construction above, and the creation of a pedestrian level above the street upon which the buildings would front. Thus it was necessary that the plan be very detailed to guide the private developers of individual parcels. But in addition to this necessary detail, it was also decided to be very specific as to the precise uses and size and shape of the structures. Thus the capacity of each office building was determined very closely, and its shape, height and precise location carefully prescribed. In addition, a time schedule based upon market absorption was established so that no private developer would be hurt economically by the throwing of too much space on to the market at one time. The development of the plan was under the direction of an architect-planner who, even though he has moved to another city, continues to supervise its execution.

The first parcel in this project was offered subject to the restrictions I have mentioned. Several developers submitted bids, and the best bid was determined on the basis of the design of the building. The architect was Mies Van Der Rohe. The building is now very nearly 100 per cent occupied and is a handsome structure indeed; what is more, it obviously fits precisely into the plan for the Charles Centre area. Other buildings, including a Federal office building, are under construction, the pedestrian level is partially completed and functioning, and the whole area is proceeding according to plan. There have been modifications in the plan, but each has been supervised by the original architect-planner. As a result there has been no tampering with the plan's concept nor have there been changes for expediency's sake. The integrity of the plan has been maintained.

The principles embodied in this successful urban-renewal project are first, a detailed design plan for the area; second, continuity in the review process; third, the selection of private developers on the basis of adherence to the design plan and on the excellence of the design submitted rather than on the value offered for the land; and finally, a strategy aimed at achieving well-defined, particular objectives formulated by the community and adopted as basic public policy.

A somewhat similar approach was used in the Erieview project in Cleveland, Ohio. Here the urban-renewal area was laid out with a basic emphasis on the design concept but without a detailed design prescription. Continuity was provided by retaining the architectural-planning firm that conceived the original plan to guide the city in the selection of developers and in the carrying out of the plan. Here the concern was to make sure that the plan emerged as intended, by having its creator work closely with the developers and their architects. This did not mean, of course, slavish attention to the original plan, for conditions do change and not all contingencies can be foreseen; but it did mean that plan adjustment was consistent with plan concept. Basic to this operation was the authority of the city to prevent construction until it had approved the developer's plans, and the availability of the designer for consultation after the plan was completed.

A major downtown project that has been eminently successful, though it has not had the benefit of the controls described in the previous two projects, is Constitution Plaza in Hartford, Conn. In this instance, the plan did not have much in the way of a design concept. Design was provided by the developer—a major insurance company interested in creating an area of good design. The basic objective of the city was to revitalise the downtown area by making land available adjacent to it. With the advent of the insurance company, the basic development scheme became private rather than public, although the city was in accord with what the insurance company proposed to do. As a result of the development, another major insurance company has decided to stay in the city rather than move to the outskirts and has erected a major new building in the project area. The lesson from this situation is that one cannot always be so lucky. Hartford was fortunate.

Society Hill in Philadelphia, Pennsylvania, is another example of strong public direction in both the design and the use of an urban-renewal area. Here, of course, one recognises the strong hand of Ed Bacon, executive director of the Planning Commission in Philadelphia. Prior to offering land for development, the Planning Commission engaged architects to develop a design scheme based upon a programme of providing apartments for upper-middle-income families, rehabilitating existing town (terrace) houses of architectural importance, and building new, contemporary town houses around the high-rise structures. The developers were selected on the basis of their design schemes, and the scheme selected did not agree completely with the original concept, but the Planning Commission felt that it was an improvement. In the execution of this project, a design review board was established to look at the developers' plans in detail to make sure that they adhered to the design concept. The result—construction is well along—will be one of the outstanding renewal projects in the United States.

One cannot discuss urban-renewal projects in the United States without mentioning the South-West Washington DC project. *Architectural Forum* has called it *the* outstanding renewal project, but others are not quite so enthusiastic. This project, as you know, is very large—about 500 acres overall —and it has been under construction for a good many years. This paper cannot detail its long history, so oversimplification and generalisation are necessary.

When the project got under way there was an overall plan for the area which was more two-dimensional than three-dimensional. It was based on zoning-type controls, and parcels of land were delineated for particular uses. It prescribed the orientation of the high-rise structures and the interspersing of town houses with commons in the intervening spaces; and basically this is the concept that has emerged. But the plan as originally adopted by the city has been modified from time to time as conditions have altered; the concept has been changed to provide for a higher density; some streets have been realigned in order to reflect the design ideas of subsequent architects who have worked on portions of the plan. The result is not unpleasing, but there is some question as to the planning and architectural unity of the area.

The design of individual structures and the site planning of individual areas is of a high quality. A good deal of this is the result of relying upon a jury of architects and planners to recommend the best layouts proposed by individual developers for particular areas, and of relying also upon an architectural review panel that passes upon the design of the individual buildings. But it lacks the design continuity built into the process in Charles Centre, Society Hill and Erieview. Perhaps its very size militates against a similar process.

There has also been little city direction on the objectives to be sought in the South-West Area. With"changing membership on the Planning Commission and on the Board of District Commissioners, there has not been a single strong thread of basic social or architectural objective available to guide its development. In fact, the question of the purposes for which urban renewal should be used is a matter of serious debate in Washington—a situation not uncommon in other cities of the United States.

One small project, not yet under construction, is particularly noteworthy in this discussion because of the unusual way the public officials determined how the area was to be developed. This project, also in Hartford, Conn., is very small. The city established a programme for X number of housing units, Y number of square feet of commercial area, and Z number of square feet of public open space. The developer was selected on the basis of site plan and design. Here the city relied upon the design competence of the architects retained by the developers to create an imaginative plan. The result was successful.

A project that has a basic social objective is Eastwick in Philadelphia. Here is an area of some 3,000 acres, low-lying, close to the city airport, and only sparsely developed with slum or blighted housing. The city's object was to develop much of this area for lower-moderate-income housing and the balance for industrial use. The city spent some little time developing a sub-division (estate) plan, though when the land was offered the developer was selected on the basis of his design, which was not the design worked out by the city. But a major requisite was that housing be built within the reach of a particular income group. The area is now being built, the houses are within the reach of these families and many of them are occupied.

There are, of course, many other examples. But I would like to use but one more. This is the Capitol Hill project in Nashville, Tennessee. The area surrounding the State Capitol used to contain some of the worst slums imaginable. When it was cleared a new street system was installed and the resulting parcels were put on the market. Controls in the plan were of the zoning type—height, density, setback, etc. There was no design concept as such. The sale of the parcels was assigned to a competent real-estate broker. As a result the parcels have been sold on the basis of developer need, with no attempt to determine the character of what was to be built. The result is something of a hodge-podge of various-sized buildings of varying height and of varying architectural style. What could have become a magnificent setting for the remodelled State Capitol has become a somewhat better-than-average development of new offices and apartment buildings.

What, then, are the conclusions that can be drawn from these examples as to the elements that are important in the urban-renewal process if it is to be used as a positive tool for the reshaping and the reorganisation of our cities— conclusions that should be relevant to any major project, whether it is urban renewal or virgin-land development in the countryside?

First and of utmost importance is the setting of a basic objective or objectives for the project. Good luck may result in a project's achieving certain goals determined after its initiation, but the chances weigh heavily against it. Where there is no clear public objective, the project becomes but another real-estate operation that does not take advantage of the opportunity created by the city in assembling acreage for a major development. At times it is difficult to obtain a clear definition of a project's goal, for its objective may be a matter of vigorous public debate, or the makers of policy and decisions may fail to recognise the importance of the tool that has been given them. Important as the clearance of the slums is *per se*, it is equally important to establish the objective of the rebuilding.

The second conclusion is that there must also be a process whereby the public officials or their representatives can give positive direction to the execution of the plan. It is not enough to rely upon the standard zoning controls to guide development; there must be a mechanism with built-in continuity to be sure the concept is realised.

Thirdly, there must also be a mechanism to provide for orderly change in the plan to meet changing market conditions and to take account of those elements which may have been overlooked in the original plan. It is very seldom that adjustments do not have to be made. In making these adjustments, it is important not to lose the original concept or to alter it in midstream so that the result is a hodge-podge.

Fourth—and this is major—is the emphasis that should be given to the role of these projects or developments in carrying out broad city objectives. There should be a general concept of what needs to be done in the city, how it should be restructured, how it should grow or change, etc., and the urban-renewal projects should then become, in part, the tools for carrying out these objectives. Since they can be controlled in a positive way they should become instruments for carrying out the city's comprehensive plan. In the States we are approaching this process through the development of community-renewal programmes aimed at creating a body of knowledge that will permit the decision-makers to select among alternative courses of action and thus establish major objectives for city development. The result ideally is a carefully meshed programme of public improvements and developments that are geared to specific needs in terms of both objectives and time sequence. But although we are approaching this in some of our more sophisticated cities, we still have a long way to go.

Fifth—and this is also major—is the leverage land ownership gives the city in exercising positive direction to achieve the objectives it has set itself. What is more, this system, whereby the land is publicly acquired, a development plan prepared and the land then sold or leased to private developers for use in accordance with the plan (and with careful supervision of what is built), has many advantages to private enterprise as well as to the public authority. It is difficult for private developers to acquire suitable land. When they do they must gear their development to the size and shape of the parcel and exploit it to the limits allowed by the zoning ordinance. In addition, they have little protection against what neighbouring developers may do. If, however, the developer acquires land in an urban-renewal-type project where he knows in advance the development scheme of the entire area, where the parcel delineated has definite relevance to what is to be put on the land and where he knows it is a part of the city's development scheme, he is well protected in many ways. He does not have to scurry about trying desperately to assemble a land parcel of sufficient size, and he knows that his building will be protected from capricious architecture or land use by his neighbour. He knows what the development plan will permit and what it precludes. He knows also that the rest of the development will actually be built. As a result, the city can expect to attract the long-term investor type of developer rather than the speculative, short-run type. Stability and quality will be more likely to result in this kind of development. As a caveat—upon which I shall not elaborate— this kind of publicly directed development does require particularly able civil servants. Public direction does not *ipso facto* result in good development. It requires able men to carry it off.

Finally, I want to address myself to the regional problems of development, since up to now I have dealt basically only with in-city developments, although many of the principles for particular schemes apply to schemes wherever located, in the city or on the periphery.

When dealing with the region and its development, we must think of new governmental devices to get around the multiplicity of local government units. This requires a regional planning operation and a regional development operation that can deal with the factors that shape the growth of the region. We have developed some regional planning bodies, but we have not yet really developed a body that can serve as the decision-maker for regional development and at the same time see that those public developments that govern the growth and shape of the region are not only actually built but are built in the proper places.

In getting at the impediment to rational regional development caused by the multiplicity of local government units, I gather that the British are not confronted with the same kind of problem as are we in the States. We have an ideological aversion to what is termed 'metro' by its opponents—to any governmental device to deal with the region on a rational basis. We also have a tendency in the States to think in terms of extreme alternatives, the 'metro' alternative being the abolition of existing local municipalities and the creation of a super single government for the entire region. In fact, rational development of the region requires a body controlling only the major developmental factors, such as the location of major roads and transport lines, the location of major utility lines, broad determination of land use and acquisition of open space. With these factors under the control of a regional government of sorts, we should begin to establish the mechanisms for rational development.

But in addition to some governmental unit overseeing these determinations, it would be desirable to have also a mechanism comparable to the urban-renewal mechanism. If there were a land-development authority for the region, it would be possible for new towns to be built through the process of land acquisition, plan preparation, installation of the necessary utilities and public facilities and disposal of parcels of land through sale or lease for development by private developers, who would have to develop in accordance with the plan and subject to the review of the local development authority. Such a land-development authority should also have the power to undertake key development schemes comparable to urban-renewal projects in both the built-up and the expanding areas of the region. This land-development authority would thus become the executing arm of the regional governmental body, providing the mechanism to carry out, in a positive way, the development plan for the region. It would clearly have to have the power of land assembly.

Perhaps other mechanisms can be suggested, but it is essential that some mechanism for carrying out the plan be established; otherwise the plan itself will have no real force. There must be a creative, positive means of achieving it. The prescription outlined here is not an easy one politically in the States, and perhaps it is not easy politically in Great Britain, but I for one can see no effective alternative, since we witness every day the ineffectiveness of plans where there is no mechanism for their execution. Plans have a way of bending and stretching, according to the pressures of the moment; and this is particularly true where the planning body is not the body that has the authority to carry out the major elements of the plan.

The time is past when we have the leisure to debate what the urban scheme should be. The decisions are at hand—in fact they are already passing us by. We are rebuilding and expanding yesterday, today and tomorrow. We must establish the machinery to give direction to regional development even though we may not be able to agree on what the form of the development should be. The debate on the means of controlling and directing regional growth and development must get under way.

Mr Bor then gave a paper describing his authority's plans for the renewal of Liverpool.

Introduction

The Merseyside conurbation straddles the mouth of the Mersey; its population in 1961 was nearly 1,400,000, of whom over half, 745,000, lived in Liverpool. This conurbation provides a classic example of a renewal region, being an area of former prosperity which, having experienced a decline, is now fighting back. The conurbation has always been dependent on industries associated with the cargo-handling activities of the port and on organisations which developed to handle the trade of the port, such as banking and insurance.

The enlargement of world trade horizons in the nineteenth century resulted in the swift growth of Liverpool, and this has left a vast legacy of slums and obsolescent areas. Changes in world trade, and in the development of British trade in particular, led to an economic decline in this formerly prosperous region, culminating in the massive unemployment of the inter-war years, which still persists, though at a much lower level.

History since World War II

With the opening of the Mersey Tunnel in 1935 migration to the suburbs on the Wirral peninsula gathered momentum. From the 1930s onwards strenuous attempts were made in Liverpool to relieve the economic problems of the region. Industrial estates at Aintree, Speke and Kirkby were established and attempts were made to draw firms into the region. Vauxhalls (General Motors) and Fords have since been attracted to Merseyside, but a much greater effort will be required in the future to provide adequate employment opportunities, to keep pace with the high rate of natural increase of the population and to reduce any further drift to the South.

During World War II Liverpool was the main gateway to Europe from the U.S.A. and Canada. As a result there was heavy war damage: nearly 26,000 houses were destroyed or seriously damaged and 400 industrial concerns were destroyed.

The need for comprehensive town planning went largely unrecognised for seventeen years. This resulted in virtual stagnation, while solutions to the regional problems of traffic, planning, redevelopment and economic resuscitation continued to be inhibited by the lack of any regional planning authority.

However, the need for the comprehensive replanning and swift rebuilding of Liverpool was at last recognised by the City Council in February 1962, when it appointed Messrs Graeme Shankland Associates as consultants to prepare a redevelopment plan for the central area. This appointment was followed up by the creation of a new city planning department under my direction at the beginning of 1963.

Although Liverpool, by far the largest city in the conurbation, has embarked on an ambitious programme of urban renewal, the city planning officer is supposed to plan only for the area within the city boundaries. This city is, of course, an integral part of its dependent conurbation and its surrounding region. Such are the difficulties and local jealousies that the local authorities on either side of the Mersey could not even agree, for instance, on the siting of a second tunnel under the River Mersey, and the Minister of Transport had to intervene. However, there is a possibility of a change in the offing. The Local Government Commission for England and Wales is currently studying the local government problems of South Lancashire generally, and the Minister for Trade, Industry and Regional Development, in conjunction with the Minister of Housing and Local Government, is preparing a regional study for the North-West.[1]

The new challenge

The very vastness of the problems of obsolescence in the city and the slowness of post-war redevelopment combine to offer unique opportunities for the radical remodelling of Liverpool and its region. One-third of the 28,000 acres comprising the city of Liverpool and two-thirds of its central area are to be renewed by the turn of the century.

Urban renewal will be based on a new comprehensive transportation system. The planning together as an integrated whole of land use, traffic and buildings will be based on Buchanan principles. The creation of a primary and secondary network, containing environmental areas in which pedestrian

---

[1] Since taken over and published by the new Department of Economic Affairs.

and vehicular traffic will be separated from each other, is being investigated.

Within the city, renewal is now proceeding with determination and speed. Slums are being demolished at the rate of 1,700 a year, and this rate is being increased to 2,500 a year, which would result in the clearance of all pre-1875 dwellings by 1981. The building programme is being increased to 5,000 dwellings a year. Large-scale peripheral expansion affords the opportunity to build new towns within the city. At the first of these, Netherley, construction is shortly to commence. But the needs of the city region are staggering: some 200,000 dwellings, equivalent to a second Liverpool, are required by 1981. This tremendous need offers the opportunity to redistribute population and employment in such a way as to form a new city region served by a new comprehensive transportation system.

Within the city region two new towns are planned. At the first of these, Skelmersdale, which is to cater for 50,000 people (of whom some 37,000 should come from Liverpool), construction of dwellings and factories has begun. The second, Runcorn, will provide dwellings and facilities for another 50,000 people, 30,000 of whom should come from Liverpool. Proposed expansions at Widnes and Ellesmere Port will provide for a further 34,000 Liverpool citizens.

Central area

Liverpool, whose central area is the hub of the Merseyside conurbation and the regional centre for two million people, is the first major city in England to produce a draft City Centre Map in accordance with procedures laid down by the Minister of Housing and Local Government in 1962. This map takes the form of an interim policy and progress report on the work of producing a comprehensive three-dimensional plan for the whole of the city centre. The draft map is designed to inform the population generally and special interests in particular of the planning ideas behind the plan, and also, by encouraging their comment, to enable them to take an active part in producing the final plan.

The planning of Liverpool to date

a) The planning consultant has, to date, produced ten reports. They describe how a square mile of the Central Area will be contained and defined by an elevated inner motorway closely associated with high-capacity multi-storey car parks. New office blocks built over some of these car parks will provide for the expansion of the city's business district, whilst other car parks will serve the main shopping precincts. Reports describing the redevelopment of certain areas of the city for office, shopping and residential purposes indicate the function and form of multi-use, multi-level building complexes which are

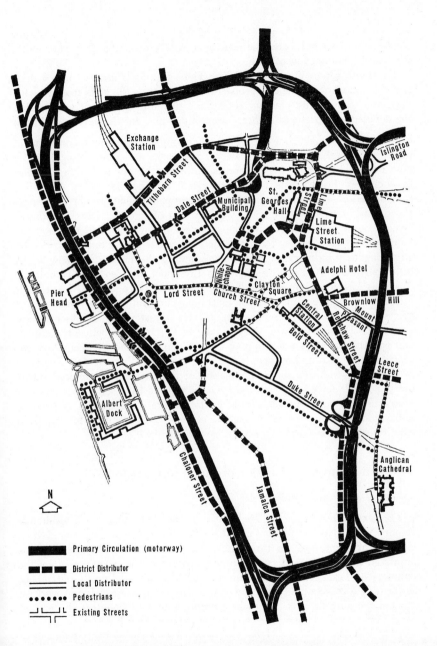

Liverpool: Proposed central-area circulation systems.

likely to be typical of the remodelling of the central area as a whole. Within the heart of the central area the pedestrian will be separated from the vehicle for the ultimate benefit of both.

The tenth report shows how the previous proposals dovetail into a draft plan for the whole of the city centre. This now forms the basis from which a new joint team of city planning officer and planning consultant will develop the detailed, comprehensive three-dimensional plan for the new central area.

b) Inter-professional teams within the city planning department, consisting of planners, architects, traffic engineers, sociologists and economists, have by now prepared fourteen policy reports outlining the main planning policies for the renewal of Liverpool within the context of the city region. A detailed transportation study to establish future traffic patterns and to check the proposed road network is now under way at a cost of £75,000. Investigations of future employment patterns in the city region have revealed that 200,000 more jobs are required by 1981, of which 100,000 will have to be provided by attracting new industry. A report investigating the factors influencing the future structure of shopping centres in Liverpool has also been completed. A survey has commenced of industrial firms in Liverpool to estimate their future land requirements and the location factors influencing the choice of new sites. Detailed studies of offices, service industry and warehousing are envisaged. These reports on the economy of Liverpool recognise the important part the city plays as a shopping, cultural, entertainment and employment centre for the two million people in the city region. Two reports have been prepared in which the future population of the city and the region and its housing needs have been estimated. Other reports have set out methods of examining the social problems and environmental inadequacies of existing housing areas within the city in the face of the growing demand for improved conditions and the rapid increase in car ownership.[1]

Detailed examples of major projects in Liverpool

A *Central-area 'traffic architecture'*

1 *The Inner Motorway, etc. (The Traffic System)* The planning consultant's Report No. 7 made proposals for a new £32,000,000 inner motorway system, elevated over most of its three-and-a-half-mile length. This scheme was approved by the Council on 2 January 1963, and has been agreed by the Ministry of Transport and the Ministry of Housing and Local Government as forming a reasonable basis on which to continue detailed design work; it will be the subject of a Bill to be submitted to Parliament at the end of

---

[1] The Liverpool City Council has since adopted proposals for the revitalisation of the railway commuting system and has published a comprehensive *Interim Policy Statement with Maps*.

1965. Closely associated with the motorway is a series of high-capacity multi-storey car parks, which will aim at the ultimate provision of something like 36,000 car-parking spaces.

A flyover will ease considerably the present congestion at the Mersey Tunnel entrance by lifting the local central-area traffic over the tunnel through traffic, and by providing a grade-separated interchange between these two types of traffic.

The street system within the motorway will be primarily for the use of buses and delivery vehicles; two road construction schemes are planned for the early improvement of this secondary road network. The Roe Street/Hood Street improvement scheme will form a new one-way traffic arrangement, and new major bus stopping points at the rear of the existing shopping streets will assist the eventual pedestrianisation of the main Bold Street/Church Street/Lord Street shopping area.

2 *Strand Street/Paradise Street* This proposal for a new central-area community was initiated by the planning consultant in association with the city planning officer and was approved by the City Council in April 1963. The development will take place on a twenty-acre site stretching from Paradise Street to Strand Street immediately behind the Lord Street shopping precinct. Rising above two multi-storey parks for 2,500 cars over an arcaded extension to the city's shopping and entertainments centre, tower blocks of flats and a lower block of 'scissor-type' maisonettes will house some 2,500 persons. At ground level, with access by escalators and lifts to the shops, car parks and residential community above, will be the new central bus station. By concentrating this multi-use, multi-level development upon the northern half of the site, a new major public open space of over six acres will also be created as an integral part of this project.

3 *St John's Precinct* The details of this £10 million scheme for the redevelopment of a site adjacent to the heart of the city's shopping centre by private developers, Ravenseft Ltd, were approved by the Council in October 1963. Design work by the architects is now nearing completion, and a temporary market has been in operation since March of this year to accommodate the traders from the old St John's Market, who have been displaced because of its demolition to make way for the scheme.

The scheme will consist of a multi-level building complex with complete pedestrian and vehicular separation. It will include a new retail market, a supermarket and two floors of retail shops, giving a total shopping area (excluding market stalls) of over 250,000 sq ft gross, together with five licensed premises, a cinema, a ballroom, an hotel and multi-storey car-parking accommodation. Incorporated into the redevelopment will be the two existing theatres, the Playhouse and the Royal Court.

4 *Civic and social centre* This scheme, proposed by the planning consultant

in association with the city planning officer and approved by the City Council in April 1963, envisages the centralisation of all the main civic functions into one area. The site for this centre is adjacent to the existing civic and social core of the city, around St George's Hall and St John's Gardens, where the existing facilities would most naturally expand.

The development proposed, again on several levels with separated pedestrian and vehicular movements, consists of a building form kept comparatively low in order to preserve the important views across this part of the city to the impressive group of buildings at the Pierhead. The centre would accommodate the local authority offices and committee rooms, professional chambers, law courts and public and private assembly rooms. These buildings would be constructed on a pedestrian podium over car parking and vehicular servicing areas and would create a new centre for civic and social life.

B *Living with the motorway*

The Cathedral Precinct This scheme for the erection of approximately three hundred dwellings and the restoration of the St James Cemetery has been prepared by the city planning officer's urban design team. The project is significant in that within an area of some twenty acres it has been necessary to reconcile the massive scale of the existing Anglican cathedral and the proposed Inner Motorway, elevated to some forty feet above ground level, with the needs of a residential community on a site falling from east to west towards the motorway.

In order to prevent the noise and fumes from the elevated motorway from interfering with good residential amenities two solutions are proposed: single-aspect housing backing on to the motorway where east and south aspects can be achieved, and where this is not possible a heavily planted embankment against the motorway with a generous open-space buffer between it and the housing. The rest of the housing is grouped in units around vehicle mews, which provide access to car parking at a standard of one space per dwelling plus a small proportion of visitors' parking. Pedestrian and vehicular movements about the site are on separate circulation systems and linked pedestrian-access decks allow a maximum building height of five storeys without the extensive use of lifts.

Each dwelling unit will have its own private open space in the form of an enclosed patio garden. The design of the dwelling has evolved from the need for small-scale compact housing with the maximum amount of privacy. Despite the considerable difficulties of the site a net density of some 120 habitable rooms per acre is achieved.

The main pedestrian approach from the city centre is diagonally to the main porch of the cathedral through a shopping centre under the motorway by means of stepped paved courts leading to formal paved platforms abutting the cathedral, with fine views across the city. Vehicular access and parking is mainly from the perimeter of the site and provision for coach parking will be made under the motorway.

c Rehabilitation and redevelopment

Abercromby area pilot project A pilot study of rehabilitation and redevelopment is at present being carried out by a housing research and development group attached to the University's Department of Architecture and supported by a generous grant from the Rowntree Trust. The area now being studied by this group for rehabilitation lies between the Anglican cathedral and the University Precinct and contains many terraces of architectural interest. An extension of the life of most of the buildings in this area would achieve not only an improvement in housing conditions but also the preservation of some of the finest remaining examples of eighteenth- and early nineteenth-century domestic architecture in Liverpool.

The group will also study the redevelopment of the housing which will have to be renewed; a pilot housing area is included in the study area. The intention is to work closely with the Ministry of Housing and Local Government group dealing with industrialised housing and to relate the development of new housing types to the overall layout. The various departments of the Corporation are co-operating closely with the group in their work and the eventual completion of the pilot development schemes will be assisted by the fact that much of the land is already in the ownership of the Council. The reports to be produced by this group will undoubtedly be of considerable assistance to the city and any other authority undertaking similar tasks.

d A new town within the city

The Netherley project In addition to the two new towns—Runcorn and Skelmersdale—which have been designated to help meet Merseyside's over-spill needs, more land will be needed on the periphery of the city if a vigorous clearance programme is to be pursued. Work is due to start in the near future on one such major scheme, at Netherley on the eastern outskirts of the city. This will provide for a population of about 20,000 people; the layout will allow for full pedestrian-vehicle separation and one car per family. An important feature will be a major district shopping and commercial centre, which will be connected to major distributor roads and will serve a total population of about 100,000 persons. Much of the catchment area will lie in the outer suburbs of Liverpool, which are at present underprovided with shopping facilities of this scale and character. Provision is also to be made for office and light industrial employment. It is hoped that the Netherley district centre will provide a viable, and preferable, alternative to the out-of-town centre, which is often physically divorced from the community it serves.

Other centres, comparable in scale and function, will ultimately replace the ribbon-shopping areas which flank the major traffic routes. The pattern which will emerge in the city region is one of a compact, specialised city centre, relying to a great extent on efficient public transport links to all parts of Merseyside and beyond, supplemented by major district centres in the suburbs and towns of the region.

Conclusions

Liverpool, second largest port and third largest city in England, has made a dramatic leap forward during the past twenty-nine months. Thanks to the Council's decision in February 1962, to make a belated but determined effort

:::::::: Shopping

━━━ Class 1 and Trunk Roads

||||||||| Social Groupings

▓▓ Principal Traffic Generating Areas

N

Liverpool (i) Existing main roads;

Shopping

Motorways

Limited Access Arterials

Social Groupings

Principal Traffic Generating Areas

N

(ii) Possible future primary network.

to change the image of Liverpool, Graeme Shankland Associates and my planning team have been given this unique opportunity. We have so far produced only broad outlines for the main new functions, forms and communications of a renewed Liverpool. Much remains to be done to develop these outline proposals into firm building projects. The greatest need, however, at this point in time, is the speedy setting up of effective machinery which would ensure that the city's bold renewal projects are closely integrated with a comprehensive transportation plan and an overall renewal policy for the whole of the Liverpool city region.

Introducing his paper, Mr Bor observed that in Britain there were more legal and administrative safeguards than in America to prevent renewal programmes from causing excessive hardship to the people displaced from the cleared slums. Professor Rapkin commented that many of the problems and difficulties arising in American urban-renewal schemes were due to a failure to take into account the complex network of personal relationships and living patterns which they disrupted. Urban renewal often meant the replacement of overcrowded conditions by more expensive low-density housing with a higher rateable value, with the result that many of the former residents had to find homes elsewhere. So far the Negro community had borne the brunt of this upheaval. But the racial difficulties experienced in any project were as much a matter of caste and class as of colour. Middle-class Negroes, who were steadily increasing in number, were more vocal when they were moved from their homes, or found their ambition to own their homes frustrated. When told they must move, many old people, small shopkeepers and small firms found they could not afford new accommodation; the financial assistance given in cases of hardship did not cover all the costs involved. In undesirable areas difficulties were often encountered, when a site was cleared, in getting people interested in its redevelopment or in persuading people to come and work in the new buildings.

8

IMPLEMENTATION: NEW TOWNS

The following account of the Reston New Town now being built in the Washington urban region was given by its developer, Mr Robert E. Simon.

The Reston Plan is for a balanced new town, related by its geography and its concepts to the national capital, to be built on 6,800 acres—900 acres of which are reserved for research and development plants, light industry and governmental agencies, with the balance of the acreage designed to accommodate housing, shopping, education, recreational and religious facilities for 75,000 people.

Reston, like other present-day new towns in the United States, is being developed by private enterprise, and in order to be completed as conceived, must of necessity be a financial success. The concepts which have been developed for Reston may be relevant to new town planning in general.

Goals of the developer

The beginning of a plan for a new town must be philosophy and not topography, zoning ordinances, public financial regulations or other factors dealing with the money market. The developer must determine his own philosophy, select his approach, list his objectives in order of importance and constantly insist upon preserving his programme. Where an objective low on his list collides with one higher on the list, the less important objective must yield.

For Reston, the objectives in order of priority are three:

a) That the people who live or work in Reston should have the widest possible opportunities to use their full potential of mind and body.

b) That it should be possible for any who want to remain in this single community to do so throughout their lives. Changes in circumstances of age, family composition or financial situation should not make uprooting inevitable or even preferable.

8

c) That the importance and dignity of each individual should be considered superior to the importance of the community.

The role of the developer or chief administrative officer

The chief administrative officer and developer of a new town must be the man who has worked out the guiding philosophy for its plan and procedure. He cannot successfully delegate his responsibility for creating concepts or enforcing their implementation to any individual or firm.

His interest in people, and in how the new town he is planning will affect their lives, is what will determine the initial shape of the community. If it is genuine and deep, it will give him the strength to resist the many pressures from professionals and technicians which attempt to infringe on his order of priorities. For this he needs to have a broad range of interests.

Use of consultants

It takes a sizeable number of widely diverse skills to plan a new town. Initial planning—probably all major planning—should be done through consultants, and implementation and co-ordination by staff. The success to date of the Reston Plan stems in great part from the use of the services of the country's best land planners, architects and landscape architects, engineers and lawyers, economists and social planners concerned with health, education and recreational facilities, in addition to experts in such special fields as traffic, graphics and lighting. Patently it is impossible for the developer to have on his staff talent in any way comparable to the skills available from consultants and specialists working with varied clients and communities.

Co-ordination of new town planning with local government

A major resource for new town planning is the community and county in which it takes place. Early inclusion of representatives of the community or local government in planning sessions, and good communications at all appropriate levels, are indispensable for the building of a new town. In Reston an enormous amount of time was spent working with the officials and citizens of Fairfax County and the State of Virginia. Out of a programme for working together on a basis of mutual respect has come acceptance of the premise that any existing statutory or procedural obstacles to excellence will be eliminated.

The Reston Plan required revision of the county master plan and a significant amendment to the county zoning ordinance. These were accomplished by unanimous vote of the seven-man Board of Supervisors. At present a committee is at work to revise outmoded procedures in streets and drainage for the benefits of all builders in the county. The School Board has accepted a grant from the Educational Facilities Laboratory for the design of Reston's first elementary and intermediate schools.

The 1967 capital budget for the county library system provides $650,000 for a branch library in Reston. Our hospital consultant, working with county and state health authorities, is preparing a plan for Reston's health complex. State agencies made the feasibility studies which preceded the impounding of water for a thirty-acre lake and provided 30,000 fish for stocking the lake when it was completed; they tested the soil at the spot selected for the first garden plots; they have contributed to the recreational programme; and the state provided 10,000 seedling evergreens planted out by our forester to implement his soil erosion and forestry renewal programmes. Both the University of Virginia and Virginia Polytechnic Institute have become involved in Reston, the former standing ready to provide extension courses in the community centre, now under construction, the latter co-operating with us on an urban agent programme.

Consideration of the desires of the individual residents

Planners frequently spend too little time on the latent aspirations for living in the community they are planning, too little time on the people who will bring their plans to life. They are likely to lose sight of the human element in discussion of design concepts, modules, questions of ideal densities, percentages of open space. Translate these ephemeral professional matters into human terms and they come into sharp focus. The focus is on people.

Reston's physical plan springs from its concept that people come first. The pattern for distribution of dwelling units reflects this. The usual pattern places the highest concentrations in a central core with density decreasing in stages out to a low-density perimeter. The result is that most residents are separated from major recreation areas. Reston's desire to make these areas as accessible as possible to all residents sparked the Whittlesey and Conklin Plan for a high-density sinew that winds its way from north to south through most of the length of the tract. This plan brings all residents within walking distance of the recreation areas.

Making open space usable

Reston's open space is based on what Lewis Mumford terms its 'social function'. Impressively large open-space areas on a master plan too often prove disillusioning. At Reston, open space is planned for because it is needed by the people. Each acre will have a purpose; if a space is open, it is not by default but by plan.

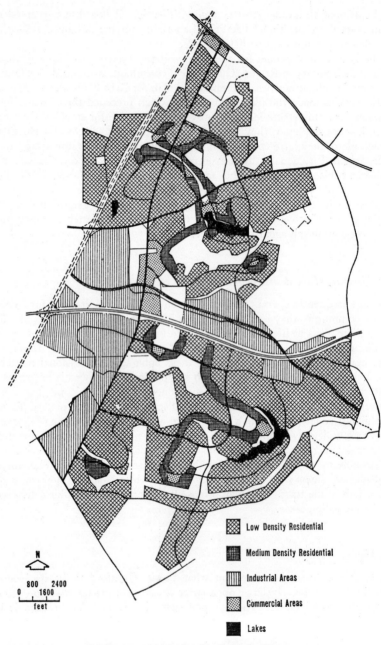

Low Density Residential

Medium Density Residential

Industrial Areas

Commercial Areas

Lakes

N

800   2400
0   1600
feet

Outline proposals for land use in Reston.

Mixed use of land

Many months of intensive work have gone into devising the right mix of housing types for the make-up of our residential communities. We do not consider this mix to be final. For us, the best mix seems to be roughly 15 per cent detached houses, 15 per cent high-rise apartments, with the remaining 70 per cent in town houses and garden apartments.

In working on specific neighbourhoods it has become apparent that each housing type profits from intermixture with the others. Our second phase of development, now being planned, makes even fuller use of the intermingling of all three housing types than does the first phase, now under construction.

Protection of privacy

For the 15 per cent of detached houses, built by individuals or builders on lots which they purchase, we have developed a small device which has large repercussions. It is simple enough—just a circle and a square—but it protects individual householders against misguided building next door. The circle drawn on each lot plan represents the area within which two-thirds of the residential structure must be built; the square shows the spot where the service area for the house is located. Each man can build his house with the comfortable assurance of knowing exactly where his neighbour's house and services will be. To date, there has been not one objection to this part of our programme from the twenty or more individuals and builders who have already signed land-purchase contracts.

Attracting employment

The problem of attracting industry in the United States is probably more difficult than in Britain because decisions on plant location are entirely voluntary.

It is too soon for us to know whether we shall have an employment centre to match Reston's residential capacity. Initial efforts to communicate the concept of Reston to industrial leaders and government officials augur well for the success of this part of the Reston Plan. Our location is an asset; Reston is eighteen miles from Washington, D.C., and lies between it and the new Dulles International Airport. Our aim is to attract research and development plants, light industry and government agencies to Reston through its various advantages as a residential community. Employers are increasingly conscious of the value of offering their staff a good place to live.

Diversity of architecture

I believe that the feeling of suburban sprawl comes not so much from the

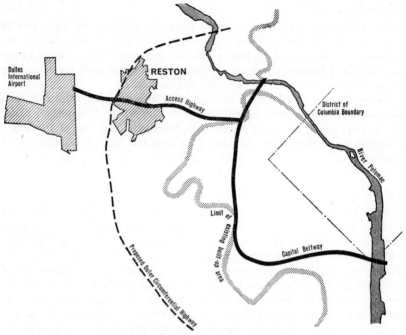

Reston in relation to Washington, D.C.

broad strokes of a master plan as from the detailing of neighbourhoods within it. An answer to the indignity of suburban sprawl is the provision of diversity by the use of a number of distinguished architectural firms—five are participating in our first village. This has created diversity which is more expensive than mass-produced sameness. The town (terrace) house—intrinsically less expensive to build than the detached house due to savings on roads and utilities—brings our costs down to compete with comparable mass-produced detached houses. On the other hand, their cost is still somewhat higher than similar town houses built in unending repetition.

Will the market bear the additional cost of diversity and lively variety? We are curious to get the answer.

*

In conclusion, I should like to give full credit for the debt we who are planning new towns in the United States owe to Britain. It is there that the fullest experience and experimentation to date have been obtained. We are constantly studying this experience and, while not assuming that it is applicable in its entirety to the United States, we have been able to gain much from it.

In reply to questions Mr Simon added that there were now twenty new town projects afoot in the United States. In the case of Reston, few banks were prepared to put money into the scheme because of its pioneering nature, but a total of $33 million had been borrowed, chiefly from the Gulf Oil Corporation (which was to provide the new town's filling stations). Reston's objective—which he did not regard as paternalistic—was to give its residents the maximum opportunity to live a full and active life. To this end he thought it necessary to avoid architectural uniformity. Since the developers recognised that they were engaged in a learning process, their approach throughout was empirical: the master plan was therefore no more than an outline sketch and the detailed plans were made just ahead of their implementation.

They had found that people would rather have next-door neighbours of a different race than of a lower income group: one of the first houses in the new town had in fact been bought by a Negro. They were not yet sure how the fact that people of different income groups did not want to mix was to be reconciled with the principle that all who wanted to live in Reston should be welcome. Some sort of quota system might prove necessary to achieve satisfactory social integration. The first 227 town houses cost from $23,000 to $45,000, with a mean of $37,000, but by 1980 the overall average price would probably be between $26,000 and $27,000 at 1965 values.

Britain's new and expanded towns were the subject of the following paper by Mr Wyndham Thomas.

The main purpose of the new towns in the urban regions (or city regions) is to assist a redistribution of the region's existing and anticipated population and employment[1].

The London ring
The eight[2] new towns around London were proposed in the Abercrombie Greater London Plan of 1944. The Abercrombie Plan covered an area of

---

1 Administration, land acquisition powers and financing of development corporations are described in Appendix 1. A list of the new towns giving their target populations and progress is given in Appendix 2.

2 Basildon, Bracknell, Crawley, Harlow, Hatfield, Hemel Hempstead, Stevenage, Welwyn Garden City.

2,600 square miles, with a pre-war population of ten and a quarter million. Because of concern over inter-war movement of people to the London area from the old industrial and rural regions, and political agreement that this movement ought to be halted by improving their economic structure and employment demand, the Plan's first proposal was that the population of the London region (i.e. the Plan area) should not be allowed to rise above the pre-war figure. (It was generally assumed at the time, and up to the middle 1950s, that the country's population growth would be slight, so that significant regional increases would come only from migration.)

The second proposal was that inner London should be rebuilt at substantially lower (though still relatively high) densities, and the movement out promoted of one and a quarter million people, with their employment:

125,000 to fringe estates twelve to sixteen miles from central London
260,000 to expanded towns twenty to forty miles out
380,000 to eight new towns twenty to thirty miles out
160,000 to expanded towns beyond the Plan area
214,000 by random addition to towns in the Plan area
100,000 wholly outside the metropolitan influence.

The remaining objectives were the prevention of further employment growth in London save in special cases; the establishment of a metropolitan green belt to prevent further outward growth of London; and the improvement of transport links in the region.

Thus the new towns were only one part of a four-part policy: the green belt to halt continuous metropolitan growth, new towns and town expansions to accommodate the pressures which made the green belt necessary, redevelopment to better standards of congested inner districts of the city, and effective control of employment location.

By the end of 1964, 300,000 people will have moved (or have been born to parents who moved) to the eight new towns. About 80 per cent of the migrants are from London. New factories in these towns employ over 80,000 people. Another 60,000 are employed in local services. Thus the great majority of wage and salary earners work in the town they live in. There is relatively little commuting to central London, but a growing interchange between the new towns and their neighbours.

Population limits for some of the towns have been or are being revised, and they will probably be called on to accommodate another 200,000 migrants. In the 1980s, therefore, their total population will probably reach 650,000, their sizes ranging then from 30,000 to 130,0000.

As they grow they complement and in some cases supersede older towns in the outer metropolitan regions as local employment centres, and in the later stages as centres for various services and entertainment. Since none of the new towns is yet more than two-thirds complete in its physical equipment, their full role in the economic and social life of the London region is conjectural. No assessment has been made of the potential of the new towns as major sub-centres of the region, nor has policy been directed towards making them such. But the potential of the larger ones (70,000+) is clearly substantial and there exists already a danger that their employment potential will be too great for a normal growth rate to be achieved in the foreseeable future. It is one of the planning dilemmas that while new towns are needed in the London region to help solve its internal problems, they do in fact enhance the region's economic and social attractions relative to the rest of Britain. Almost every one of the first 300 industrial firms (there are now 500) to move to the new towns has since expanded at least once, and many of them several times. The environment is so superior to that in most old industrial towns of the north of England, Scotland and Wales that many of the vacancies in local service employment are filled by people from these areas.

Houses and apartments built by the development corporations are allocated to employees of incoming industrial and commercial concerns, and to those filling vacancies due to the expansion of local statutory services. Almost all the dwellings are rented, but a growing number are being built for sale on ninety-nine years lease. Vacancies in local employment are as far as possible filled by recruitment through government employment exchanges in London of people having the requisite skills, being in need of rehousing and wanting to move to the new town. Were employers allowed to recruit labour freely with rental housing readily available, much greater movement in from the rest of Britain would have resulted.

In recent years there has been some private house-building in some of the new towns, either on land sold by the development corporations or on land allocated for housing in the master plan and bought from the private owner by the builder. In practice it is impossible to secure that these houses are occupied by people having a local employment tie. The builder operates in a market, he fixes his price and sells to the first buyer. But this partly vitiates the aim of creating a town to help solve London's housing problems, so it is not being strongly encouraged.

The new town method

It may appear to outside observers that 'more new towns' is British planning's stock response to the problems posed by urban growth and increasing congestion. But the truth is that the wide powers available under the New Towns Act, the fact that large financial deficits can be carried, and the ability to become monopoly landowner as well as planning authority for its area make the development corporation an extremely effective instrument of public purpose. The combination of powers, finance and a clear development directive imparts considerable drive to any corporation, even one of modest competence—provided it is given a realisable task. These inherent advantages have led to the use of the new town procedure for wider purposes than just accommodating big-city surplus population and employment.

The new towns related to Glasgow serve this purpose, but also strive to attract new employment into the region, and with considerable success. By this means they help to create new employment in a region of relatively high (over 4 per cent of the working force) unemployment.

Livingston, the latest of Scotland's four new towns, is intended to serve as a major economic growth point of this kind, while still assisting Glasgow to reduce population in its grossly overcrowded tenement districts. *Runcorn*, south of Liverpool, will have a similar role. But here (as at *Redditch*, near Birmingham) there is already a sizeable town needing large-scale redevelopment which could not readily be executed by the district council or the county council (the statutory planning authority). *Dawley*, west of Birmingham, and *Washington*, south of Newcastle, will have the added task of clearing land left derelict by mining.

The new town method is a far more effective way of organising rapid and comprehensive development than the one other method tried—expansion of established towns under the Town Development Act. This relies on a tripartite agreement between a city wanting to reduce population and a county council and district council wanting more people and, primarily, more local employment in their area. The agreement has to be approved, and is then modestly grant-aided, by the Minister of Housing and Local Government. The process is cumbersome, the relationships delicate and changeable, and the financial basis inherently weak. Prospects seem best in those places where the three authorities have set up machinery and given financial underpinning in an attempt to secure the advantages now enjoyed by the new town development corporation. But no significant contribution to the solving of metropolitan region problems seems likely from this pattern.

The private-enterprise new town seems no more likely to make a contribution. In the first place it is very difficult to start. The complete and continuing public control of land use which is the basis of British planning inhibits the developer's initiative. He can build only where he is allowed to build, so before assembling a large area of land he must be assured that planning permission will be forthcoming. To avoid paying values inflated by such a permission he must secure the assurance in advance so that he may secure the land in advance. This would look like collusion and might prove politically intolerable.

Given a resolution of this difficulty, a private enterprise project would have one great advantage here that it is denied in the American context: the much stronger development control powers of a British county council would enable it to prevent other building in the vicinity—which is the great threat to the proposed new town of Columbia, between Baltimore and Washington. But as with Columbia and Reston, private enterprise projects are possible only in regions of rapid growth, and then only in the localities of that region with good roads to the central city. The private project could bring ordered growth in an area which would in any case grow, but it could not directly assist (unless a public building agency were also involved) in solving the housing problems of the central city's low-income families. It would cater for middle-income families at a higher level of income and to an even greater extent than the present new towns around London. (It may not be appreciated that the new towns are, compared with the country as a whole, socially unbalanced in quite the opposite direction from that generally assumed. They have a preponderance of lower-middle and middle-middle-income families. It would in fact be a valid criticism that they have given too little—almost negligible—help with the housing of the poorer families of unskilled workers in London, and perhaps in Glasgow.)[1]

Introducing his paper, Mr Thomas dealt with some stock criticisms of the new towns:

1 *London has continued to grow* This is not a fault of the new towns, which have successfully carried out their original purpose of accommodating the London overspill beyond the green belt.

2 *The new towns are not big enough* It is the function of new towns primarily to provide employment for their inhabitants; particularly in the case of those near London, they are not expected to cater for the more esoteric tastes of their populations. As they grow they acquire normal town facilities.

3 *The architecture of new towns is drab, dull and visually uninspired* There is some truth in this accusation but it should be remembered that the new towns had to be built in the shortest possible time and at the lowest practicable cost.

4 *The inhabitants often become neurotic* Some people who have moved from a big city may well experience difficulties and tensions hard to overcome in the early period. They find their surroundings unfamiliar and the rents high. But the great majority adjust quickly and very few take more than a year to settle down. In any new community there are bound to be transitional difficulties, but those in the new towns are minor ones.

The lessons which have so far been learned from the new-town developments are various (Mr Thomas added). The minimum size should be 40,000 to 50,000 in order to justify the time and expenditure

---

1 See also the Appendices to this paper, pp. 184-8.

needed to create and maintain a development corporation and to provide public services, such as schools, and reasonable shopping facilities. In the future there may be a need to think in terms of larger numbers—up to 250,000—concentrated into a highly articulated cluster, and to organise within it the widest possible diversity of homes and environment. We should avoid going into a project with the pre-conception of an even spread of building; our planning should be a liberating process which increases the range of choice. On the subject of investment there is a need for increased public intervention in order to establish a platform for private initiative that would be to the ultimate benefit of the public. A competent Act of Parliament, with the right finance and machinery, can generate its own dynamic, as the New Towns Act has proved.

9

DEVELOPMENT VALUES
AND CONTROLS

The seminar's next field of inquiry was the relationship between land value and the planning and control of land use. Mr Winnick opened this session with the following paper.

One of the most neglected subjects of modern economics is the theory and measurement of urban land values. This neglect is all the more astonishing in view of the important, even critical, public policies that are dependent on an adequate understanding of land prices and the reasons for their change. Needless to say, the past fifty years, and particularly the past twenty, have seen the rise of an elaborate structure of land-use policies, controls and laws —zoning, urban renewal, highways, open spaces, new towns—all of which take as their starting point the fact that urban land is a scarce economic good for which there are competing demands. Yet it is no exaggeration to say that land value theory still rests pretty much on the Ricardian analysis of differential soil fertility to which could be added some heated comments by Henry George and some useful insights by Robert Murray Haig on the rise and fall of aggregate urban land values. We would also acknowledge some important contributions by urban geographers (particularly the Germans) on spatial organisations of economic activity. Nonetheless, in all of Alfred Marshall's *Principles* only a very short chapter and an even shorter appendix are given over to a rather dispirited discussion of site value; the same disinterest is observed in the standard American and British economic textbooks. Whatever discussion one does find is usually related to agricultural land or to the real property tax, the latter likewise a subject by-passed by the present generation of economists and only recently being reclaimed.

Because theory has lagged behind policy, the latter has often taken a wrong turn, sometimes very wrong. There is, I believe, a vast overstatement of the overall tax gains to be derived from urban renewal, of the long-run costs of providing open spaces in congested city centres, and of the wastage of land given over to the automobile. Likewise, I think that many if not most zoning ordinances have elements of economic irrationality, partly because zoning laws are local and deal with micro-economies, partly because economic relationships between the size and shape of buildings and the size and shape of sites are not yet well understood, and partly because continuing changes in transportation, consumer preferences and construction technology make for rapid obsolescence of those few facts we already possess.

As I have said, urban land values arise because there are competing uses for given sites. This competition is inherent in an economic society. Land values are independent of type of ownership, whether public or private, and arise in a socialist as well as a capitalist economy. In a market economy, land values are made explicit and are expressed by prices. But land values, as I will illustrate, are implicit even when sites are allocated by non-price mechanisms such as administrative regulation. As long as each unit of land is different from every other, as long as these differences are unique and cannot be costlessly duplicated, and as long as the stated differences have economic significance—in that different sites will lead to different amounts of consumer satisfaction or cost reduction or revenue yield—unequal demand will be created and a bidding process will get under way.

For example, even in the very simple organisation of the venerable European weekly market, differential land values (or their equivalent in the form of rent) arise because some vendors prefer certain sites over others. The favoured sites may be on the shadier side of the square or closer to the main stream of consumer traffic. Likewise, even in a non-market economy such as the Soviet, there will be many more demanders for sites in Moscow than in other urban settlements of comparable physical size and, within Moscow, more demand for some locations, perhaps closer to the Kremlin, than for others. Land values may, of course, be suppressed and allocations made by some other means—perhaps by custom or by seniority or by degree of party loyalty or by lot. But suppression of land values does not mean their elimination. Urban land value will crop up in some other guise—as the implicit value of seniority or of party affiliation or of a lottery ticket, a value which comes about because of extra market sales or reductions in transport costs or the glow of added status. For any or all of these benefits some potential users are willing to pay.

In Yugoslavia, for example, where urban land is nationalised and is allocated by non-market methods, differential site values come about in the following way. Under Yugoslav rules, when a collective enterprise in Belgrade wishes to build housing for its workers it is required also to provide a new dwelling unit for any family that is displaced when it takes possession of the site. Those sites for which there is the greatest demand for new housing tend also to be those most densely occupied by existing structures—that is, the strongly preferred central locations are the most crowded. Consequently, an enterprise that wanted a site in the inner ring of Belgrade might have to displace as many as sixty families, whereas it could obtain a site farther out by displacing only twenty families, or one in the vacant areas of the suburbs without displacing anybody. To house a hundred workers the enterprise that wanted the central location would have to pay the cost of building 160 dwelling units, while the next preferred site would require them to build 120 units and the least preferred site only 100 units. Since construction costs amount to about $10,000 per dwelling unit, the central site has a presumptive land value $400,000 higher than the next preferred, which in turn is worth $200,000 more than the vacant land in the suburbs. Socialist economy or not, nationalised land or not, there is present here an array of differential land prices only thinly disguised.

Neglected as the current theory of land value is, we are still better equipped to explain differential land values (Ricardo's problem and that of the ordinary real-estate appraiser) than to explain aggregate land values (the quest of Henry George and Robert Haig, and—as I have just learned—of British town planners). There are, to be sure, remaining weaknesses in our understanding of differential land values. But these weaknesses are present in the theory of demand in the market for any good or service—our inability to forecast, to know which are the appropriate capitalisation rates to apply and to come to grips with powerful but non-measurable consumer motives such as the search for status and prestige. It is easy enough to establish differential land values whenever two alternative sites are associated with different cost or revenue possibilities—provided we are confident of the correct rate to use in capitalising given cost savings or revenue gains. But we are without much knowledge of the consumer's reasons for seeking, and of what he is willing to pay to obtain, a more satisfied view of himself and a better aspect to others—two very dominant forces in the market for residential land and increasingly for commercial land. It is not possible to explain away the much higher site value of 76th Street and Park Avenue compared with 96th Street and Park Avenue by capitalising (at any feasible rate) the extra savings in time and money of a shorter ride to work. Likewise, Morningside Heights is much more favourably located with respect to the time-cost of a journey to work than is Gracie Square. Yet residential sites in the latter area are two or three times as valuable as in the former. Likewise, it is doubtful that many firms could claim cost savings or revenue gains equal to the differences in land value between a Third Avenue and a Fifth Avenue office location. Prestige and other non-measurable factors—increasingly important as we become more affluent—render less applicable Haig's theory of urban land values. Haig's thesis that land values come about from the friction of space —the economic cost of transporting people and goods—is most useful but incomplete.

But the greatest gap in theory and measurement has to do with aggregate land value rather than with its relative distribution. (To put it in another way, there is no adequate explanation of the base line of land values from which the relative values are scaled.) The aggregate of urban land values may be likened to a mountain whose mass can be distributed in a variety of forms, sometimes as a sharp-peaked pyramid, sometimes as a truncated cone, sometimes as an irregular series of contours with odd-shaped bumps and lumps and valleys. But how is the mass itself explained? Surely, the aggregate value of urban land is determined by factors different from those that determine its spatial distribution.

For example, one has no trouble in seeing that if a theatre has a certain supply price (rent) this aggregate can be distributed in various ways depending upon the differential demand for each seat. Because of human limitations in seeing and hearing (and because, more and more, of our old friend, status) the first six rows of the orchestra tend to be more highly priced than the next six, which are in turn more expensive than the balcony, and so forth. (Likewise, the aggregate rent of, say, an apartment building will be distributed according to the relative desirability of the high floors over the low floors and of front views compared with back). But, given certain assumptions about the degree of competition in the theatre industry, the aggregate rent for a theatre would depend principally on such exogenous factors as whether or not the play is a hit and the reputation of the performers, rather than upon the particular distribution of prices within the house.

In the example of the food market mentioned earlier, whatever the differential values of each particular site, would not the aggregate rent established by the owner of the market site be determined by the number and purchasing power of consumers? As long as consumers come to the market with a relatively fixed schedule of food wants dictated by their incomes, family size and tastes, the real-estate owner, given some degree of competition in the market for land, could do little to influence his aggregate rent, no matter what changes were to be effected in the distribution, say by doubling or halving the number of food stalls or by raising the rent of one stall and reducing that of another. The aggregate rent payments necessary to bring into being the requisite number of theatres or food markets would have little or nothing to do with how this rent was internally distributed. The forces which determine the aggregate seem to rest on factors quite different from those which explain the contours.

I have nothing very useful to say about the variables that are presumed to govern aggregate land values (or rents) other than to raise a series of questions. The mass of urban land values is clearly related in some fixed way to the aggregate level of annual rents families and business firms are willing to pay and the rate at which these rents are translated into capital values. There is no other source of value. But how is the mass affected by changes in economic activity or by shifts in the mix of expenditures in favour of land-consuming sectors, say if consumers divert purchasing power away from food and towards housing? On this we have not much to say. Will, as Professor Haig argued, the mass of values be reduced as the technology of transportation improves or, as Alfred Marshall diffidently suggested, as building technology permits higher structures with lower land coverage? Probably, but not certainly.

I would, however, contend that it is because of the confusion between aggregate land value and its geographical distribution that public policy most often goes astray. The most common error of all is to assume that a gain or loss in value at a particular site is accompanied by an equivalent gain or loss in the aggregate. Let me give some examples. American urban-renewal programmes frequently assume that real-estate investment in redevelopment areas will result in a proportionate gain in real-estate value, and therefore in real-estate taxes. How many times do urban-renewal officials tell us that for every dollar of public subsidy towards land write-down there will be five dollars or ten dollars or one hundred dollars of private investment and for every dollar of local subsidy there will be five dollars or ten dollars or twenty dollars gain in real-estate tax revenue? These assertions are based on an economic fallacy: namely, that supply creates its own demand, that every hundred dwelling units built in an urban-renewal area represent a net gain of one hundred new dwelling units to the aggregate housing investment of the city, metropolitan area or nation. This is patently untrue. New housing is too expensive a commodity to be purchased impulsively or out of a patriotic desire to support the municipality's urban-renewal objectives. The families that occupy the new housing units in an urban redevelopment area came into the market because they had certain housing wants; most if not all of these families would have purchased or rented new units elsewhere in the city or metropolitan area. Indeed, one of the most cherished objectives of urban renewal—to keep middle-income families from moving to the suburbs or to bring back those who have left—is a clear concession that there would be little or no gain to the metropolitan or national housing inventory or real-estate investment or real-property tax yields.

A city can, of course, gain at the expense of the suburbs but even here there is exaggeration to the extent that most moves—four out of every five—of central-city residents are not to the suburbs but to another central-city location. (Indeed, the market for apartment houses, the most frequent type of new housing in renewal areas, is so different from the market for one-family houses that relatively few of the families in urban-renewal apartments, the overwhelming majority of whom are childless adults, are likely to become migrants to the suburbs.) Similarly, when a city like New Haven develops an urban-renewal site with a huge new department store complex it is difficult to believe that there is much if any increase in aggregate retail sales or aggregate retail-store investment. Any added retail sales in New Haven's centre are at the expense of other retail stores, some in New Haven, some in adjoining communities. I do not mean to say that urban renewal is not justified even if the aggregates are unaffected. Quite the contrary. A most persuasive

9

case could be made why there should be more retail sales and more middle-income families in the declining inner rings of the metropolis than in its mushrooming outer rings. But the urban-renewal programme is not helped by resting it on faulty premises and extravagant promises.

One could point to similar errors in assertions made by highway engineers who take gains in land values along a new highway route as net increments in the aggregate without taking into account the losses in real-estate values along the old highway as existing restaurants, filling stations and motels decline, or of the value gains that would have taken place at various other sites if the new highway had never been built.

Another illustration of the error that results when the part and not the whole is observed is the clamour that has arisen in connection with such massive structures as the Pan American Building—almost universally condemned as a monster of congestion that adds 25,000 new people to the Grand Central area and chokes the streets and subways. Here again, it would be highly unjustified for us to assume that firms rented space in the Pan Am Building simply because it was there. It is more realistic to believe that the demand for office space arose out of fairly deep-seated business needs (including the demand for a prestige location). Had the Pan American Building not been built, an equivalent or nearly equivalent amount of office space would have been built elsewhere in the Grand Central area. Congestion in this area, where all subway stations and streets are about equally crowded, would be just as great or greater if the 25,000 workers emerged each day out of six ten-storey buildings instead of one sixty-storey building. Indeed, by providing direct access to the subway and by providing internal lunch rooms, the Pan Am Building may have on net balance reduced the uses of scarce outside street space. (Recall Marshall's suggestion that bigger buildings decrease aggregate land values, i.e., decrease the overall quantity of land demanded.) The problem of congestion in Grand Central may be a genuine one and perhaps public policy in New York City, as is the case in London, ought to do something about redirecting new office buildings to less densely occupied sections of Manhattan or the metropolis. But one must recognise that the size and shape of a particular building affects little if at all the aggregate amount of office-building space required to support urban activity.

A third illustration is the frequent claim by public officials that they cannot afford to provide small parks in open spaces in the central districts because to do so would remove valuable land from the tax rolls. If the demand for office and consumer space is determined by exogenous factors, would not the pre-emption of a block or a part of a block for a park simply shift the demand for space elsewhere in the city, probably very near to the original site? For instance, were the site of the Stock Exchange Building in New York taken over as a park, the Stock Exchange would almost surely re-establish itself (as it is in fact about to do) a little distance away. The total amount of economic activity, from which all land value and therefore property taxes derive, would be little if at all affected. To the extent that the Stock Exchange would be replaced by a new and more expensive structure, total real-estate taxes would indeed go up; though, to be sure, this gain would be offset by the non-recurrent cost of the enforced taking (accelerated depreciation) of the older building. I do not wish to overstate my case or to imply that the heedless pre-emption of sites given over to specified economic activities may not result in a genuine reduction in economic efficiency by stretching the distances between linked activities, or in a permanent loss of these activities to the city (though less probably to the metropolitan area, and almost not at all to the nation). But I would insist that the critical variable to be looked at is the impact on overall economic activity, not the change which takes place at an individual site.

I do not wish to over-extend this paper by taking on further controversies with those who, like Professor Vickery, wish to ascertain the full cost of using automobiles in crowded cities by imputing a rent for street space. Usually a high cost is calculated, but these high costs are derived by attributing the same value to streets as to the land under the adjacent office buildings. Such a calculation assumes that doubling the quantity of land available for office sites would lead to a doubling of the quantity of office space built—a rather incredible assumption, since at going land prices the demand for office space has been in balance (or even over-balance) for some time.

Measurement of land values

I do not know whether the points I have made in this discussion paper are useful or not. I do know that whatever views are offered and whatever rebuttals are made, any serious discussion of the problem is crippled by lack of systematic empirical data on urban land values. I cannot think of any important economic sector that is so lacking in cross-sectional and historical information on prices. Such fragmentary data as we do possess are based on little more than hearsay evidence. Did we not read that the Empire State Building was sold for so many millions of dollars, of which such and such was attributed to the value of the land? And again did we not hear at lunch the other day that the corner of Madison Avenue and 49th Street was sold for $200 per square foot? These rumours and rumours of rumours are supplemented by other bits and pieces of uncertain quality from deed recordings and from FHA annual reports, and from an occasional study of one neighbourhood or city by an appraiser (valuer) or doctoral candidate.

The difficulties of assembling an adequate body of data on land prices are inherent in the nature of the market for real estate. Real estate is a highly individualistic business. People do not often tell other people what they actually paid or received in a real-estate transaction. Further, transaction prices, even for the same parcel of real estate, may be highly variable, depending upon the particular (and the usually confidential) terms of trade. A parcel would sell at one price for cash, at quite another if there were available a high-ratio, low-interest mortgage, and at still another price if the transfer of the fee (freehold) were encumbered with long-term leases.

But most important of all is the fact that every piece of real estate is, in principle, unique, different if only by a little from every other. As is well known, the theory of price indices rests on the premise of a high if not perfect degree of interchangeability in the units being traded. What makes matters worse is that urban land is often, if not most frequently, traded as a joint commodity where land and building are merged. I do not want at this time to get into the controversy whether land values can ever be separated from building values. But it is clear that even if one were to agree that such separation is theoretically valid, the practical problems of making the required adjustments would be enormous. Any effort to subtract from total transaction price the net value of buildings which are seldom alike in size, design, age, and quality, would leave large relative errors, all of which would bear heavily on residual land values.

Despite all of this pessimism, I believe that something approaching an objective index of land prices is possible. Such an index could be constructed along various lines. One method, which has already been experimented with, would be to assemble data for a sizeable number of real-estate transactions and then to return to the record books to reconstruct historical data on transactions for the *same* set of parcels. The percentage changes in price between the time intervals could then be computed and averaged (whether the average should be weighted or simple would constitute a fine question). The advantage of such an historical index would be that we would be dealing with presumably identical parcels subject only to (perhaps) more or less regular process of ageing.

A second technique would be to adopt a panel of representative types of real-estate parcels and to follow their transactions as they occur in the future. Or both methods could be combined, working backwards and forwards. One would have to recognise, however, that it would be no easy matter to define, much less to gather, a representative sample or to maintain its integrity in a market where transactions are relatively infrequent.

Let me end my paper at this point, conceding that I have not done justice to the importance of the subject. I am not sure that I have put the main lines of my argument as clearly or as completely as I had hoped to. I have also given scant attention to the reciprocal effects of land value on economic activity—for example, to the ways in which the price of land affects the nature of economic processes by imposing certain constraints on the size and shape of buildings (high buildings are more expensive per unit of space than low ones), by requiring less efficient vertical flows of people and goods, and by producing such intense land-conserving and land-sharing adaptations as to increase congestion, i.e., the time and cost of movement. Nor can I wholly refute an argument that in some degree the supply of real estate does create its own demand, that some firms are prompted by the erection of a new office building to take a harder look at their existing arrangements, or that an urban-renewal project may accelerate certain investment decisions or that some investors may act philanthropically to abet public policy goals. The omissions and inaccuracies in my arguments only reinforce the need for economists and statisticians to return to a subject now left to the superficialities of real-estate appraisers and the almost total disregard of city planners.

Dr Lichfield agreed with Mr Winnick that the neglect of land values by economists—in Britain as in America—was deplorable. He also agreed that an action which increased or diminished the value of a particular site did not increase or diminish aggregate land values to the same extent; indeed, it might only change the distribution of land values without affecting their aggregate at all. But he insisted that it did not necessarily leave the aggregate unchanged: in the phrase used by Sir Arnold Plant in opposing the 1947 Planning Act, 'there is no law of the conservation of value'. If energy in one form was suppressed it would reappear in another, but land values that were suppressed in one place did not necessarily crop up in another. For example, if the demand for office space in the best location for that purpose were frustrated, and alternative sites in less attractive locations were offered in lieu, aggregate land values would be diminished. Conversely, if land values were enhanced on one site it did not necessarily follow that they would correspondingly decline on another, or that a rise in values that would otherwise have occurred elsewhere would be correspondingly inhibited. It was therefore possible for good planning to increase aggregate values and for bad planning to diminish them; but he agreed that the extent of the increase or diminution in value must be measured over the whole of the area affected by the planning decision, not merely over the site that was being planned.

Dr Lichfield also had reservations about Mr Winnick's view of the difficulty of isolating the land component in the market value of a piece of real estate. Since the 1947 Act British economists had accepted a distinction between the value of a piece of land in its current use and its value in a potential use. The financial provisions of our planning legislation had been based on the general understanding that there was one value which attached to a piece of property if it was to remain in its existing use and another which attached to it if it were to be used for development. Indeed, this distinction was illustrated by Anglo-American differences in the system of local taxation: in Britain a man paid rates according to the value of his property in the way he used it, while in America he was taxed on its potential value.

As to the problem illustrated by Mr Winnick's example of the Pan American Building over Grand Central Station, British speakers agreed that if one had to decide between erecting a large new office block at a terminus for commuter rail services and building it in a commercial zone half a mile away, there was a strong case for choosing the former site so as to minimise street congestion. But if this decision were taken in pursuance of a policy to limit total office employment in the city, and therefore entailed the refusal of permission for an office building in the commercial zone, the owners of land in that zone would under British law be entitled to some compensation for the loss of their opportunity to gain from its use for office development or redevelopment. Moreover, this compensation would have to be paid from public funds which would have no share in the financial benefits reaped by the developer of the rail terminus site. Given the principle of full compensation for all restrictions on the right to continue an existing use of land, there seemed to be no way of giving effect to a regional plan aimed at reducing metropolitan congestion, short of buying up the whole central area and so being able to extinguish uses where they were not wanted while reaping the benefit of their redistribution.

This led to a general discussion of the financial arrangements that should be made to deal with the problems arising from the fact that development control inevitably altered the distribution of land values, whether in the aggregate it increased or diminished them. If it was accepted that compensation should be paid to owners who were adversely affected by this redistribution of values, should not 'betterment' be collected from those who gained from it? And if so, how?

The following paper by Dr Lichfield reviewed the history of British attempts to tackle this problem.

Introductory—the twenty years experiment

Britain by now has almost twenty years' experience of the most comprehensive system of land-use control yet seen in a non-socialist country. This system was initiated in the Labour government's Town and Country Planning Act of 1947. Until 1953, when its dismantling began, it included a comprehensive solution for the compensation-betterment problem—that is, the problem of making financial adjustments between landowners and the community to compensate for the redistribution of land values which flows from land-use planning. From such wealth of experience, it might be thought, Great Britain will have found the answers to compensation and betterment in a property-owning democracy. But this is not so. While our machine has solved certain problems it has found new ones. And after twenty years of debate and experiment we are once again in a ferment of controversy over the land problem which is reminiscent of the 1940s. Suggestions for new solutions are being made from sources right across the political board. That of the Labour Party is of particular interest, for it could well be in power again late in 1964 after thirteen years of opposition, and it has pledged itself to the early implementation of a bold new programme which is quite different from anything tried before—in short, a programme of nationalising land required for private and public development.[1]

Against this complicated background, the most useful contribution of this paper, it is thought, will be to describe our present system and its evolution from the 1947 Act; to show how certain major land-use and land-value problems have been solved; and to enumerate the problems which are causing anxiety, and which await the next experiment.

Contrasts in American and British public controls over land use

But before proceeding it will be helpful to indicate the essential similarities and differences in the American and British approach in these matters. Scarcity of space will, I hope, condone the reckless generalisations.[2]

The rights and obligations of proprietary interests in real estate are much the same in both countries, the American system stemming from the English common law. But the source of public rights over private property differs, giving rise to important differences in practice. This can be shown in relation to the conventional American classification of social controls over land use: taxation, the police power and eminent domain.

Taxation is soon dealt with. Whereas in America discriminatory taxation can be introduced to influence land use (for example, in partial relief to redevelopment projects of local real-estate taxes) this is not so in Britain, where uniformity of treatment is the rule.

The police power, the enforcement of regulations to preserve and promote the health, safety, morals and welfare of the people, corresponds to 'negative' controls in Britain, including development control. In practice, the scope of the control is in each country roughly similar in content. But whereas the American constitution offers unlimited scope subject only to its interpretation

---

1 The Labour Party, *Signposts for the Sixties*. London 1960, pp. 19-23.
2 For an authoritative comparison see Ed. Charles, M. Haar, *Law and Land: Anglo American Planning Practice*, Harvard University Press and the M.I.T. Press, 1964.

in the courts, in Britain each successive kind of control must be authorised by Parliament or Ministers. And whereas in America no compensation need be paid for the resultant potential or actual loss in property value whenever the police power is legitimately exercised, in Britain the liability arises when Parliament thinks fit that it should. We do not pay for enforcing minimum standards in factories, shops, etc., but we do for terminating a non-conforming use.

Eminent domain equals Britain's compulsory purchase, or what can be more correctly called enforced sale. But whereas in America the source of power is simple (the constitutional requirement for public use, which is being widened by the courts to include public purpose), in Britain there must be specific legislative authority for each kind of taking. And while the powers are simply enormous there are still gaps in relation to land-use planning. Compensation must be paid in both countries. Being less generous in disturbance to occupiers, the 'just price' of the American constitution is more severe to property owners than the current British code of market value.

In both countries, the dividing line between police power and eminent domain, and therefore in principle between non-compensable and compensable, is very tenuous and difficult to define, and is becoming more so. But a classic, and neat, American distinction seems to say a great deal for both countries '. . . it may be said that the state takes property by eminent domain because it is useful to the public, and under the police power because it is harmful, . . .'[1]

From these generalisations comes the surprising conclusion: that given the general will to use them, taken all in all, American social controls over land use are inherently no less powerful than those in Britain, and the compensation price to be paid need be no higher.

Compensation-betterment today

The system ruling since 1959 in Britain can simply, if not precisely, be described as no compensation—no betterment. How this arose can only be understood by tracing the steady dismantling of the 1947 Act financial provisions between 1953 and 1959.[2] And here again there must be generalisation.

In the 1947 Act the vital distinction was made between existing use values, the value of property for the use to which it was currently being put, and development values, the additional value for a more profitable potential use.[3]

---

[1] Ernst Freund, *The Police Power, Public Policy and Constitutional Rights*, 1904, quote. in Charles M. Haar, *Land Use Planning*. Little, Brown and Company, 1959, p. 544.

[2] The Statutes are the Town and Country Planning Acts, 1947, 1953, 1954, 1959, 1962 and 1963.

[3] To be more precise, existing use value included a minor element of the development value, the Third Schedule tolerances, but the distinction is not important for our purpose.

Existing use values, including any subsequent rises in value, remained the property of the owner. Any depreciation through injurious affection (police power) or compulsory purchase (eminent domain) therefore had to be compensated at prevailing market value: and on compulsory purchase there was paid in addition an element for disturbance to the occupier. This protection of existing use extended to the right to rebuild for the same use: while the physical act could be prevented, some rather tortuous provisions secured compensation to the owner if he were precluded from reinstatement.

But the development values received much rougher treatment in the famous 'development rights scheme'. Under this, all development rights in developed and undeveloped property were taken by the State in 1947. The government was then in a position to sell them back to any landowners who wished to develop or redevelop. The price was the 'development charge': the difference between value with and without the planning permission which was the prerequisite for the development. And, it follows, no public body needed to pay for the development rights on compulsory purchase but only for the existing-use rights.

In taking the development rights, the government argued that while at common law they had no liability for compensation, they would nonetheless set aside a global fund of £300 million for the purpose, in order to avoid hardship to property owners (and presumably to the government also). The fund would be distributed by 1953 (in government bonds) among the affected owners, on a *pro rata* basis according to the amount of loss that each had suffered at the date of expropriation, plus interest. The valuations (appraisals) to determine the loss were then put in hand. They were eventually found to total some £400 million.

But in 1952 the government announced its intention of abandoning the compensation-betterment provisions of the 1947 Act; it introduced its changes in 1953–54. It maintained the position on existing use values, which still endures today, and concentrated on the development values. Development charges were abolished and no provision for the collection of betterment was substituted. Distribution of the £300 million was forestalled. Having handed back the development rights, the government had to reintroduce compensation for their depreciation. And here, I like to think, the ingenuity of the solution showed the flair of the then Minister, Harold Macmillan. Compensation became indeed payable for restrictions on development, but in practice only when the restrictions amounted to complete prohibition of building, and not always then. And even where it was payable, the ceiling was the amount of development value (at 1947 prices) which was registered as having existed in 1948 (unexpended balance of established development value). And this registered amount was all that was paid on public purchase, in addition to existing use values.

This last provision created a situation in which an owner could sell to a private developer at a considerably higher figure than would be paid by an acquiring authority. This disparity led to the 1959 Act, which completed the unscrambling by restoring market value as the basis for public acquisition.

The 1962 Act codified the Acts of 1947–59, but only after the Land Compensation Act of 1961 had consolidated the land acquisition code, including certain provisions which had been included in the Town and Country Planning Acts, 1944–59. This was welcome in helping to relieve planning from unmerited odium connected with compensation.

Some problems solved

Summarising, we have the following situation. While the formidable statutory powers of planning and public acquisition which were granted in the 1947 Act remain much the same, and in certain respects have been strengthened, the financial provisions have been completely dismantled. The result is that the private land market is able to function reasonably freely (although somewhat wearily, for it is dependent on the planning machinery, which can be very time-consuming and arbitrary); and the authorities are able to exercise their planning functions without being entirely inhibited by possible money loss. Some of these functions, of relevance to urban regional planning, are as follows.

Police power

1 *Urban sprawl* The physical size and shape of settlements can be controlled, green belts established and the intervening land kept free from urban development, by the simple expedient of refusing permission to develop. In certain instances no compensation is payable at all, as where the development can be shown to be premature. Where compensation arises, it is payable by the State; a very significant factor for local authorities. But whatever the amount of damage the ceiling is the amount of the 1947 Act claim. This cannot be an over-formidable item in a period of rising land values.

2 *Use zoning within urban areas* Within settlements, where development is contemplated, the nature of the land use can be controlled by the authorities, without any question of compensation arising at all. This control can take severe forms. The owner of a site which has shopping potential but is on a main road might find that he is permitted to build only houses; the owner of a house with office potential might find that he cannot use it for business purposes.

3 *Form of development* Where the proposed use is not in dispute, the form of development can be controlled with great particularity without question of compensation. Here again the degree of control is severe, and can extend

to building bulk, residential density, architectural appearance and provision of car-park spaces.

Eminent domain

1 *Public facilities* Any public agency can buy land for the discharge of its statutory functions, provided the specific legislative authority exists. The price is open market value, including any development potential, plus an allowance for the loss arising from disturbance and severance. But where the affected landowner is also the owner of contiguous or adjacent land, there can be a 'set-off' in the compensation on account of any enhancement of the value of his remaining land.

2 *Public development* Where the appropriate public agency is enabled to carry out urban development, as for a new town, expansion of an existing town, or renewal of an obsolete area, it can buy as necessary. The purchase price is open market value. But in order that the public agency need not pay for the prospective value to be created by its own activity, there are provisions for limiting the purchase price. In practice these exclude some but not all of the development value to be created.

But having assembled the land, the authority has great freedom in its disposal. It can sell outright, though in practice it does not: leasehold development is the general rule. But one new feature has crept in which is of great significance: the principle of buying land compulsorily not only for direct public use or ownership but also for leasing to private developers where they are proposing to develop in accordance with a scheme favoured by the authority.

Some problems unsolved

The exercise of these planning functions, in a situation of mixed private-public land economy and no compensation—no betterment, results in a re-distribution of income and wealth which is attracting criticisms on grounds of equity. Unfairness can be traced as between at least four distinct entities.

1 *As between specific landowner and landowner* The development plan and planning permissions are paramount in deciding whether a particular land-owner reaps development value or not. Fortunes in money are often at stake, and there is no redistribution of gains or losses between landowners.

2 *As between specific landowners and consumers in new development* Rising real-estate prices must be expected in a society which is experiencing population increase, economic growth and general inflation. But the bitter pill of rising prices (and rising house prices in particular) is the more difficult to swallow

when the profits remain in private hands and when capital gains remain largely untaxed in a country with a high rate of income tax.

3 *As between specific landowners and public agencies in new development:*
  a) In new towns and expanded towns—Despite the provisions for disregarding, on land acquisition, the increase in market value attributable to the actual or prospective scheme, the existing landowners do in practice get some of the development value to be created by the authority. But they think they ought to get more, whereas the authorities tend to think the reverse;
  b) Urban renewal—The same kind of tension arises in urban-renewal projects, but it is more acute. Not only is the money involved per acre much greater but on the authorities' side there is the suspicion that there is something wrong about paying very heavily to acquire bricks and mortar of which much, by definition, is condemned as 'obsolete';
  c) In providing municipal facilities within towns—Under the market value rules, authorities are buying land for car parks, schools and open space at prices based on what developers would pay for private development if it were permitted on the site. These prices are regarded as too high. They clearly have no regard to the true value of these facilities, whatever that is, or to the betterment created for adjoining owners or the values shifted by the public development on to other land.

4 *As between landowners in general and the community* In a country with comprehensively planned land use, vast public-sector expenditures, a backlog of urban obsolescence which is perhaps the greatest in the world and no effective capital gains tax, there is special reason for doubts about the propriety of letting 'unearned increment' flow into private pockets.

These problems, as stated, are all problems of the distribution of income and wealth, and might as such be relegated to discussions on social justice in a democracy. But their significance is deeper than this. If the financial framework for land-use planning is manifestly unfair, and unduly benefits the private as against the public sector, then it must rock the land-use-planning boat. For one thing, it must tend to interfere with the allocation of land to the use which is best in the public interest. Land which would otherwise be kept in green belts is allocated for building in the hope of bringing down land prices by increasing supply. Uniform densities are permitted on neighbouring sites to 'maintain equity', whereas the locations might really demand differential densities. Public facilities are steered to cheap land in poor locations, or not provided, and urban renewal is slowed up. For another thing, the integrity and objectivity of elected representatives and officials is under strain when they have power to make or withhold fortunes—a depressing feature in a country of great traditions in its public service. And finally the bitter political atmosphere, together with innumerable cases of personal hardship, tends to defile the whole of the planning machine as the only palpable cause of the discontent.

In these circumstances the future of land-use planning is imperilled. And so, on the spiral staircase of history, we are back to the issue which produced the Uthwatt Committee: the evidence that the difficulties being encountered by planning authorities, under the then existing compensation-betterment provisions, were so great as seriously to hamper the progress of planning throughout the country. The Uthwatt analysis led to the solution, in the 1947 Act, of the difficulties of the thirties. Our current difficulties are different. But we clearly need another Uthwatt.

Speaking to his paper, Dr Lichfield said that after twenty years' experience British planners ought to be able to tell their American colleagues exactly how to deal with this problem. In fact, having unscrambled the arrangements made in 1947, Britain now had a system which nobody regarded as stable.

Development control in America was exercised by the use of three major tools—discriminatory local taxation, the 'police power' and compulsory purchase. In Britain it was thought that taxation should be uniform throughout the country, but in the United States the practice of stimulating industrial development in a particular locality by reducing the property-tax rate was accepted as a legitimate means of influencing the use of land. The power of governmental authorities to set limits, in the public interest, to the private owner's freedom to use his land and buildings as he wished was similar in scope in both countries, but there was a very important difference in its operation. In Britain, whenever Parliament introduced a negative control of this kind it had to decide whether or not any compensation should be paid to the people whose interests it affected. In America the introduction of any such control could be vetoed by the courts if they found it went beyond what was authorised by the Constitution, but once the courts had certified its legitimacy no question of compensation could arise. In this respect the American attitude to the property rights of the individual was more ruthless than the British. Similarly, the American and British arrangements for the compulsory purchase of real property by public authorities were much the same, but the American code was far more brutal in its treatment of the people displaced through redevelopment, while the British code could be invoked for a much less limited range of purposes.

The use of both the power of 'eminent domain' (compulsory purchase) and the 'police power' (negative controls) deprived the private owner of property rights. In America no distinction was drawn between a private owner's development rights and his right to continue an existing use of his property. The right to develop the full potential of one's property, like the right to go on enjoying its existing use, was subject to restriction without compensation—but only if the courts acknowledged the constitutional validity of the restriction as a necessary safeguard for a legitimate public interest. In Britain it was accepted that the government should never interfere, for either reason, with an owner's continued enjoyment of an existing use of his property rights without buying him out at market value or paying compensation for his loss; but Britain had a much less tender regard for the private owner's right to put his land to a more profitable use. Indeed, he could not do so without express permission. If he was prevented from doing so altogether, he received compensation based on the extent to which he had been deprived of the benefit of such development potential as had been attributed to his land in 1947, but he had no claim if he was allowed to carry out some other and less profitable development than the one for which he had sought permission.

There were thus no legal or administrative obstacles to prevent a British planning authority from taking almost any planning decision it wished. Its difficulties lay in the sense of injustice aroused by the operation of the existing arrangements for dealing with the consequent redistribution of land values. Economic growth and increasing population were inevitably raising the price of the land which carried permission to develop, and people thought it unfair that some landowners were allowed to make fortunes from development while others reaped only the benefit of any increase in their land's value in its existing use. There was also a general feeling that public authorities were having to pay private owners too much for the land required for schools, open spaces and other unremunerative forms of development, because the compulsory purchase price was based on the land's market value for the most profitable use to which it could have been put if it had not been needed for public use—though in the case of a new town project a global valuation determined the price paid for individual holdings. Furthermore, some people thought that where land increased in value in its existing use through no action taken by its private owner, the community should have some share in this unearned income.

It was therefore not the planning problems of the allocation of land to the best uses, but the problems of equity involved, that Britain had failed to solve. But this failure was not simply a question of social justice falling outside the planner's province, for a planning system that was demonstrably based on inequities could not work in practice. Britain was finding that because of these inequities, schools and parks were being wrongly located, density controls were getting misused and the very integrity of public officials was coming under suspicion. Until these problems were solved a stable foundation for future land-use planning could not be established.

Mr Slayton denied that discriminatory local taxation was widely used in America as a means of promoting development: only two states used tax abatements to stimulate middle-income housing and urban renewal, and there was considerable opposition to the idea in principle. He also pointed out that the acquisition of property for urban renewal was carried out under varying local laws, and he knew of no case in which a public authority had threatened to take over private property because it was badly maintained: he doubted if it could be done in the present climate of opinion. He agreed with Mr Winnick that urban renewal did not necessarily increase aggregate development and taxable values, because without it the development would have taken place elsewhere; but it did increase the tax income of the authority responsible for the central city, where demands on social services were much heavier than in the suburban municipalities, and this seemed to him politically and morally just. One dollar's worth of public investment in urban renewal might well generate six dollars' worth of private investment within the area of the investing authority. It might also induce a general upgrading of the area and accelerate the average rate of investment over the region as a whole.

Some argument ensued as to whether an attempt to collect betterment was compatible with an attempt to reduce the level of land prices. Classical economic theory suggested that a betterment levy should depress land prices; but had this tendency been reversed by the operation of the planning system in limiting the supply of land for development? Would not any levy be passed on to the purchaser? Mr Thomas pointed out that an effective compensation-betterment scheme would at least reduce the cost of the land needed for public purposes. Mr Munby said there was a good economic case for taxing all capital gains, and especially capital gains on land that were due to the decisions of planning authorities.

Mr Harris observed that in America there was always a bias towards increasing real-estate values, and a consequent distortion of the land-use pattern, because local government revenues depended so heavily on real-estate taxes. But the most efficient plan was the one that minimised land prices and transport costs by producing a distribution of uses that minimised the demand on land to accommodate movement between centres of activity. Efficiency was not the only criterion—one might want to combine it with others—but it was a criterion that had never been seriously applied in practice because of the difficulty of analysing the effects of different combinations of planning decisions over a whole metropolitan region. He had no doubt that the restriction of development over a green belt as large as London's did have a large effect on the level of land prices. The way to bring prices down was to combine three lines of action in terms of a development plan: an increase in land allocations for various purposes, large-scale improvements in the transport system and a widespread redistribution of employment opportunities to reduce the journey to work as far as was consistent with the realisation of the economies of scale and concentration that metropolitan living made possible.

Mr Wells said that in seeking a solution to the betterment problem it was important to bear in mind the reasons why the 1947 development charge had broken down. The first reason had been that the system was beyond public comprehension: one of the things that had led to the breakdown had been the suicide of a man who had invested his savings in a house plot and then found that he would have to pay a development charge as well. In this respect the situation was now completely different: property owners had become used to the idea that no development value attached to their property except by virtue of a planning permission, and a betterment tax arising out of planning permission was therefore comprehensible. The second reason for the breakdown of the 1947 system had been that the charge was fixed at 100 per cent of development value, and had therefore taken away all incentive to put land on the market for development. When the 1947 Act was passed it had been intended to vary the charge so as to encourage development where it was wanted and discourage it where it was not, but for technical reasons which had not been generally appreciated at the time this had proved impracticable. Any new solution to the betterment problem must be one that did not discourage the development of land.

Today it was almost universally believed that a solution must be found. Suggestions being canvassed ranged from complete nationalisation of the land to some form of limited betterment tax or capital levy. The Conservative party had been officially silent on this question because any policy it produced would be regarded as simply a counter to the Labour proposals; but it was under increasing pressure from its back-benchers, whose schemes were all based on the reinstatement of a development charge, though not at 100 per cent. So it looked as though the Conservative political climate was favourable to this solution. The Labour party was proposing to set up a Land Commission, empowered to acquire, at existing use value plus some addition, all land on which development was to be permitted, with the exception (for political reasons) of single plots for private houses. Land so acquired would then be leased to a private developer, at a rent reflecting its value with planning permission, or sold to a public authority at a price reflecting its value in the use for which it was needed. This, it was argued, would enable development values collected from commercial developers to be used to offset losses incurred in acquiring land for unremunerative public purposes.[1]

Mr Wells thought this proposal was ill conceived and would not work. In particular it could not achieve one of its stated objectives—to reduce the price of private housing. It differed radically from his own suggestion for a piece of national accounting machinery—that all land acquired by public authorities should pass through the hands of a National Land Finance Corporation, so that the profit made on its disposal for commercial redevelopment in central areas could be set against losses incurred in unprofitable public development.

Another scheme, put forward by the TCPA, was for all practical purposes the same as that suggested by some Conservative back-benchers. It comprised a betterment levy payable on the grant of planning permission, and amounting to two-thirds of the resulting increase in value, together with provision for compulsory purchase by public authorities at a price representing current market value less the betterment levy. This, it was suggested, would lower the price of land needed for public purposes without making the owner worse off financially than if he had sold his land for private development, and without discouraging the sale of land for development. Mr Wells thought most people now agreed that a betterment charge of this order was the right answer, and that it should be coupled with the compulsory acquisition of land on a much larger scale—particularly the land required for the large-scale town expansions projected in the South-East Study and for the comprehensive redevelopment of central areas.

The taxation of site values, which had also been suggested, could not

---

[1] These proposals have been substantially modified since the Labour party took office in October 1964.

work in Britain because the value of a site depended on the most profitable purpose for which it could be used, and this could not be known until a planning application had been determined. Taxation of the capital increment realised on redevelopment was another proposal which Mr Wells rejected, on the ground that big development companies retained the ownership of the buildings they erected, so that the capital increment was reflected in the value of their shares, and if this were taxed selectively the flow of insurance companies' funds into development would be diverted elsewhere, bringing the process to a halt.

Mr Wells had little doubt that the new town machinery was the most effective instrument of positive planning that Britain had yet evolved, and one that was now completely accepted. He was equally sure that large-scale compulsory purchase was the only way of dealing with the problem of central-area redevelopment.

Professor Mandelker then summarised, in the following paper, the potentialities for positive regional planning of the machinery now available in Britain and America.

The limitations imposed by the Federal structure of American government produce the greatest contrasts in American and British capacity to plan effectively on a regional scale. Policy-making in America is a mixture of decisions at national, state and local levels, no one of which carries with it a mandate of compulsory implementation. The national government shapes policy through financial inducements, and state governments may authorise their local units both to accept Federal aid and to avail themselves of the substantive powers necessary to carry out selected programmes. But the decision to act is local. As a result, substantial disparities exist between urban regions both in the availability and in the exercise of critical powers. Even on so crucial a matter as the setting aside of future rights-of-way for the interstate highway system there may be considerable variation from municipality to municipality over a very restricted geographic base. Contrast the comparable English statutory authority, which is contained in the national legislation, and which is implemented in every local development plan.

Nor does the distinction turn solely on the point that British planning legislation is mandatory while the American is usually permissive. British planning is run directly from the statute, and British municipalities do not legislate in the planning field in the sense that American municipalities do. Several important consequences follow, including the foreclosure in Britain of the opportunity to guide planning machinery to purely local ends. British local government administration also relies more heavily on national administrative review rather than on the judicial check. Freedom of action at the national level combines with the all-encompassing and mandatory nature of the planning legislation to permit comparatively rapid changes to meet new demands. Change in America comes more slowly, partly because state and local legislative action must always be secured as a prerequisite to the implementation of a planning programme. For example, not until 1963 did the State of Missouri adopt an enabling act authorising its municipalities to prepare land-use plans, and then it was based on a 1926 model act which fails to authorise municipal attention to such matters as open space and community development at highway interchanges.

Reliance on judicial rather than on administrative review has had other consequences in America. Judicial attention to planning issues is episodic, fortuitous, and limited by rules of judicial intervention which severely restrict the judicial impact on local land-use decisions. National administrative review, on the other hand, can be continuous, informal, and either nominally or critically effective depending on the disposition of the national administration. A frown of Ministerial disapproval might discourage a restrictive suburban policy which in America would have to await a court attack that might be delayed, and whose effectiveness would depend partly on the context in which it was raised and on the skill of counsel.

Because of these limitations on the exercise of their reviewing power, and in spite of tentative steps in some states, the American courts have been unable to provide a regional perspective that can correct local bias. In Britain, placing the reviewing power at the national level and confiding its exercise to a Cabinet department have created an effective agency for the carrying out of national and regional planning policies. For example, national legislation confides the siting of new towns to the national planning Ministry. This power is critical. To leave the siting of new towns in America to the initiative of private or public development corporations with no superintending authority would open up unlimited opportunities for unearned windfalls, and might seriously distort rather than assist the realisation of planning aims at the regional level. The failure of the courts to correct improper redevelopment agency decisions in the selection of redevelopment areas does not hold any promise of a better performance in connection with new towns.

Although the freedom of American municipalities from external review other than the judicial check has often been noted, other assumptions which underlie the basis on which enabling power is conferred have been overlooked. For example, the degree of power conferred does not vary substantially with the size of the municipality, so that the smallest fourth-class city may possess as much potential power as the metropolis. In states in which municipalities have been authorised to carry out planning and zoning outside their boundaries, the statutory extension of municipal authority to points three or four miles beyond the municipal limits can create a miniature empire out of the smallest city. In Britain, by way of contrast, the degree of power varies with the size and rank of a municipality. Both countries, however, possess inherent limitations on regional planning arising out of the character of the residual unit of local government, in each case the county. Regional intercounty planning may indeed be farther along in America, where lower densities and the interstate highway programme have led to regional planning processes spurred by the requirements of the Federal-aid highway act.

Whether more effective regional planning will have to be stimulated at the national or local level is currently under debate in both countries. The existence of advisory regional agencies in many parts of America provides the framework for further adaptation, and recently introduced Federal legislation would make the creation of a permanent regional planning agency a prerequisite to the receipt of Federal aid in any of the urban programmes. Advisory regional planning mechanisms are not impossible to create in either country; implementation produces the difficulties. None of the American regional agencies has yet developed effective powers of implementation—an important lack.

No doubt the American planning machinery interferes a good deal less with market choice than does the British, the most distinctive difference being the latter's assumption that residential uses are not entitled as of right to locate themselves anywhere in residual zones. This superficially bland assumption hides an important ingredient to regional planning, in so far as any regional plan requires underlying decisions about urban form. Any pattern of urban organisation other than a continuation of low-density sprawl must assume an arrangement in which relatively dense areas of urban concentration alternate with relatively low-density areas of open space. An example is the British strategy of dispersing metropolitan population to new towns and other growth points, which are tightly held together against a backdrop of the green belt and similar land-use policies. Exclusive zones freezing out residential uses at urban densities have not been extensively tested in America, although some recent cases cast doubts on their constitutionality. Without some such mechanism, however, even the protection of the fringes of a new town will prove difficult.

The adoption of green belts and other land-use policies which severely limit urban development also raises threshold questions about the scope of uncompensated regulation in each country. While American zoning and related ordinances can be much harsher than British planning controls, they are subject to judicial challenge on constitutionality grounds, and where they are held to be invalid there is no regulation at all. This event cannot occur in Britain, where the division between compensatory and non-compensatory regulation is carefully delineated by statute, and where the planning decision that crosses the line is compensated, though not fully. National machinery to handle the compensation problem releases the pressures that might distort the local planning programme.

To the extent that the existing American machinery realises planning aims that are expressed at the municipal level, a greater attention to regional problems will require the evolution of a new structure that is fastened on a wider geographic base. While this point has often been made clear, the continuing role of local government in the implementation of a regional plan has been overlooked. One attempt at a compromise is the British method of delegating power from county to municipality subject to county review, a technique that is under considerable trial in the newly-evolving arrangements for the government of Greater London. Whether the exercise of conventional planning powers at the regional level will be enough is another matter. Not even the stronger regulatory powers available under the British system have been fully effective as a technique for realising positive planning aims. Much of the evidence points towards greater public involvement in land development as a more effective means of control.

Public ownership of land subject to development is one solution, although it is easier to accomplish in the more compact urban settlement structure which characterises Britain. The potential of the highway network as a factor in regional growth patterns is just beginning to be recognised in both countries and American consideration of such devices as interchange control techniques is still at an elementary level. Officially approved developments, such as new towns and expanded towns, are getting a new and bigger try in Britain and are just beginning to make a meaningful impact on American thinking. One suggestion is that the public ownership of critical development points and growth areas may prove to be the key to effective regional control. In such a scheme, the potential impact of an expanded American Federal-grant programme for the acquisition of strategic open space should not be overlooked. Public ownership of critical development sites could be coupled with minimum state or national regulation to make the basic land-use allocations which implement regional policies. One model is the attempt in Hawaii to earmark recreational, residential, and non-residential development zones through administrative action at the state level, leaving detailed implementation to the localities. This analysis points unexpectedly, in America, towards a strengthening of the role of state government. Britain, on the other hand, currently debates the creation of new forms at a level intermediate between the national government and the conventional pattern of local units.

In presenting his paper Professor Mandelker drew particular attention to the tendency for administrative control to replace judicial control in the United States, and to the effects of America's lack of a rationale of compulsory purchase. Taken together, the techniques and devices available to the planner of a suburban county in America looked much more impressive than when they were considered one at a time: if used intelligently and in combination they could enable him to achieve a unified development. The real difficulty was that each pro- gramme had its own autonomous legal structure: no one agency in the hierarchy of the American system had authority to sit down and consider all the factors at once. He thought the idea of a designation order, adapted from the British system of new town development, might do much to remedy this defect. Subject to state approval, the application of such an order to a substantial area would enable the local authorities concerned to submit to the state planning department a master plan indicating where development should be encouraged, where held back and where prohibited. Thus presented as a 'package', the restrictions involved would, Professor Mandelker thought, be accepted by the courts.

Once such a master plan had been adopted, the combined use of all available tools would enable it to be carried out, with private enterprise undertaking the process of development in some parts of the area and a development corporation in others. Each local authority concerned would decide the purposes for which land in its area should be publicly acquired by the development corporation. In Britain, it was pointed out, the typical division of functions and rewards between private and public enterprise in comprehensive redevelopment areas was that the public authority, having made possible a large profit on the commercial part of the development by unifying land ownerships through com- pulsory purchase and by putting in public facilities, left the execution of the commercial development to a private developer but shared with him the surplus of profit over the return he must pay on the capital he had borrowed. Mr Slayton commented that a Republican Senator from New York had suggested a similar arrangement for urban-renewal projects.

Mr Slayton went on to agree that American planners had a panoply of controls to hand: what they lacked was some way of applying them through a governmental agency with authority over all forms of develop- ment throughout the region needing to be planned as a whole. He did not share Professor Mandelker's faith in the potentialities of the 'official map' procedure for reserving the designated route of a proposed highway and controlling frontage development. He accepted the need for an *ad hoc* development corporation to make possible the planned development of a new town, but insisted also on the need for some kind of metropolitan governmental agency to tie in such projects to a basic regional plan.

Mr John W. Dyckman pointed out that a lot of anxiety had been caused in some states by the fact that a publicly chartered development corporation in America could levy taxes on its district and leave its future residents with no freehold property interests to safeguard their political rights. He saw more hope in the operation of an urban-renewal type of development agency on a regional basis.

Questioned as to the minimum scale at which he thought the twin objectives of planned development and social justice should be pursued through public ownership rather than through development control combined with a betterment levy, Mr Wells said he thought the land should pass straight into public ownership (even though some of it might later be sold back to private enterprise) whenever it was proposed that a town should be substantially expanded and the location of the new development was known. Where only normal 'infilling' was to take place this method of collecting betterment was too cumbersome and a betterment tax was to be preferred. His reason for objecting to the Land Commission proposal, however, was not that the scale of public acquisition it envisaged was wrong but that the method was unworkable: allocated land which had already changed hands at development value in the reasonable expectation of permission to develop would have to be allowed through the net, but thereafter the number of conveyances and assessments of compensation for compulsory purchase to be made each year would be too burdensome; the assessment of a betterment levy would be a much simpler operation.

He recalled that the Central Land Board set up by the 1947 Act had also had the power to buy compulsorily land allocated for development if it did not come into the market, but this power had only been used once because the idea was too unfamiliar at the time. He did not agree with Professor Self that the obstacle to large-scale public ownership was the Treasury's reluctance to pay out vast sums in advance of requirements: local authorities were having no difficulty in getting loan sanctions for long-term projects. He did agree with Mr Ash that a betterment levy must tend to restrict the supply and therefore to increase the price of land, and that large-scale public ownership must be the main solution to the urban development problem, while the betterment levy should be used simply to take care of the problem of equity in the residual sphere of 'infilling'.

Mr Bor added that in urban renewal public acquisition of the land was necessary (and welcomed by private developers), not only because there was no other way of assembling large enough areas for comprehensive redevelopment, but also in order to secure leasehold control over the form of the development. Without that the controls available under the Planning Act were insufficient to enable planning objectives to be achieved in the complex process of urban renewal. Sir William Hart supported this view: in London, he said, the planning authority's real achievements had come through the exercise of leasehold control, not of planning controls. Unless the planning authority owned the land adjoining major road improvements it was going to have great trouble in getting them to fit decently into the urban scene. Dame Evelyn Sharp observed that public ownership was not a passport to heaven: it brought its own enormous problems.

Dr Lichfield agreed with Mr Wells that the imperfections of the land market made it impossible for private enterprise to clear sufficiently large areas for urban renewal without invoking the help of the local authority's power of compulsory purchase. The most ingenious efforts to get private owners to pool their ownerships on a large enough scale to carry out what was essentially a private-enterprise function had failed. There had at first been doubts about the propriety of the exercise by a local authority of its compulsory powers on behalf of private developers, but it was now realised that in so doing the local authority could also serve the public interest. The compulsory acquisition of land was justified not by a public *use* but by a public *purpose*. Theoretically, if all the landowners in a town were obliged by law to get together in a holding company, which would then own all the floating development values, all the purposes of public ownership would be achieved; but private owners did not have the sense to observe their own interests collectively, so the public authority had to step in and get the odium of doing the private market's job. But other speakers thought the purposes of public ownership in the planning field far transcended those which such a holding company could be expected to pursue, no matter how enlightened its view of its collective self-interest.

Professor Wibberley pointed out that unless the compensation-betterment problem was solved, British planners would have great difficulty in maintaining amenity on the fringes of the developing urban areas. Commercial agriculture had done a marvellous job in producing really attractive countryside close in to the towns, but it could not be relied upon to go on doing this now that the difference between the agricultural value of the land and its value for other uses was widening. The livestock farming based on crops and grass that created the scenic pattern around British towns could not be profitably continued with land prices well above £200 an acre. If part of the development value were taken away this might give more permanence to agricultural land uses close to the edges of towns; otherwise their maintenance could not be taken for granted.

Mr Richard May summed up the meagre results in both Britain and America of attempts to plan against the economic forces expressed in land prices, and suggested that such efforts could succeed only if their strategy was based on the use of public investment to influence land-price changes in the desired direction first. His paper read as follows.

'There is in all planning, even if it were ever so earthily rooted in comprehensive studies of facts, an element of belief in reason as an independent force in history and in the freedom of choice by which man can change reality according to his design and so turn the course of future development. In essence, planning is an exercise in a non-deterministic conception of history, though it recognises the limitations put up by existing conditions and forces and their causal interrelations.'

Gunnar Myrdal: *Beyond the Welfare State*

Prerequisite to the consideration of land-use controls is a recognition of the existing conditions and forces within our societies, and the determination of development policies consistent with this framework. For it would seem that alternatives to present trends in the shape and structure of metropolitan regions must be acceptable within the general context of the existing social, economic, and political structure, and in line with the emerging forces and governmental policies relating thereto.

A few examples of the existing characteristics of the United States framework appearing most relevant to urban development patterns are as follows:

Private land ownership and an abundant supply of vacant land.
Fragmentation of land ownership.
Fragmentation of governmental units.
Planning controls administered by the most local governmental level.
Use of police power as the primary basis for land-use control.
Low rates of assessment on vacant land.
A system of income taxation favourable to real-estate investment and speculation (i.e., rapid depreciation, reduced rates for capital gains).
With the exception of urban renewal, a system of land development guidance which is largely negative in application.
One-half to three-quarters of the cost of local government supported by the real-property tax.

Federal support of one-family home ownership by extensive mortgage insurance programme.

However, powerful forces such as the following are bringing about rapid changes in the structure:

Rapid population increase and rising longevity.

Rising incomes for middle and upper income groups, and an increasing number of wage earners per family.

Increasing permanent unemployment resulting from automation.

General increase in employment in services, with most new service jobs at metropolitan core, and with new manufacturing and research jobs gravitating to the outer-ring areas.

Increasing automobile ownership and use, but growing awareness of the need for continuation and improvement of public transport.

Increasing leisure time.

Minority groups actively seeking entry into white residential areas, despite continuing and even hardening resistance in suburban areas.

Expanding capital expenditures and aids by state and Federal governments for all types of public facilities.

Rapidly accelerating physical deterioration and increasing social tensions in older urban areas.

High residential mobility within and between metropolitan areas.

Are current British and American planning policies and doctrines in accord with these conditions and trends? Some observations bearing on this question come to mind:

1 The continuing drift of population to urban areas is a matter of concern to planners, but neither national government seems to share this concern or evinces any intention of taking measures to alter this trend. (The South-East Study, in accepting the inevitability of growth, reverses or ignores the findings of the Barlow Report.)

2 Sprawl at suburban densities in the outer ring of metropolitan areas is also a matter of planners' concern, but is nevertheless occurring at an increasing rate to satisfy expanding middle-class desires. (Again the South-East Study seems to accept the inevitable in forecasting that two million out of the three and a half million anticipated growth by 1981 will be housed by 'general absorption' in the outer ring.)

3 Automobile ownership and use for travel to work is increasing despite our expressions of concern at increasing congestion and waste of economic resources.

4 Employment within the urban centres is increasing, despite rising congestion and travel costs, because an increasing share of total employment is going into service activities which favour central locations.

5 Britain, after an abortive experiment with a system of land controls based on eminent domain (compulsory purchase) rather than police power (development control), has attempted to return to police-power controls with somewhat unsatisfactory results. Today, flexibility in the exercise of development controls is reportedly creating confusion and insecurity. At the same time the supposedly rigid control of land use under zoning in the United States is being more and more flexibly administered in practice.

6 Efforts towards official metropolitan status in the United States have been largely foiled by the militant resistance of suburban property owners and their representatives in local and state governments.

7 What has been learned from experience with the London green belt? As a container of metropolitan growth it has certainly failed. Is it now to become a device to push the outer ring of development further out? In the United States it is viewed as the symbol of British development policy, and ideas regarding its present status and future role are of great interest.

8 In both nations the pace and scale of redevelopment activities have not been sufficient to affect metropolitan patterns for a number of reasons. The relatively small expectations for rebuilding of older areas in the South-East Study and the modest requests for renewal authorisations in the United States do not hold much hope for urban change from this source in coming years.

Public investments determine land uses and land values

Under a system of private land ownership, determination of land use by governmental controls can operate only within the general limits prescribed by the economic forces of the land market. (Even the tool of eminent domain is limited to some extent by the high cost of property acquisition.) Should we not therefore aim to control or influence land values in the directions of planning strategies which conflict or run counter to the forces generated by the pattern of land values? As I learned from Sir Raymond Unwin many years ago, it is public investment which is the prime creator of land values. The accessibility and amenities created by transportation facilities, public utilities, parks, educational and cultural facilities, etc., indeed make land utilisation feasible in urban areas.

Patterns of development must therefore first be determined by public investment in line with planning strategies. In Britain, planners have been aware of this for some time and the need for government initiative is generally accepted. In the United States there is much thought along these lines by professionals, but little action as yet. In fact one might say there is almost too much thought and debate among professional circles in the United States as to planning policy. Could it be that the plethora of studies, treatises, debates and conferences among metropolitan planners are symptoms of our ineffectiveness and inability actually to affect metropolitan development? Social and political scientists can properly indulge in the search for perfect metropolitan solutions (or at least those which seem perfect for the moment on the basis of computer analysis). However, the planning profession and those in government have the responsibility to act. There are strong moves by Federal agencies towards the requirement that metropolitan areas must have plans in order to be eligible for highway funds and other aids. Perhaps leadership in addition to persuasion is needed and could be achieved by the preparation of official Federal policy reports on the scale of the Uthwatt, Scott and Barlow reports by Presidential commissions. But let us indeed proceed on the basis of some policies; for as we learn more these can always be modified, as there is a great time span between plan and reality. In fact the rate of social and economic change is so great that the policies which meet needs in one decade will inevitably require revision before the following decade is upon us.

If the present activities of state and Federal governments were correlated at the metropolitan level, and expanded in some cases, they could exert a tremendous influence on the patterns of land values and land use. Let us cite some of the significant areas of public capital investment:

1 Transportation facilities (road, rail, air, water). Grants and supervisory functions affecting routes, fares, freight rates, etc.
2 Redevelopment (urban-renewal) grants.
3 Grants for acquisition of open space, urban land reserves, etc.
4 Public utilities (water, sewers, power and fuel) grants and supervision.
5 Grants-in-aid for community facilities (schools, hospitals, etc.).
6 Aids for new or expanded community development.
7 Housing finance aids—mortgage insurance, subsidies, etc.
8 Aids to distressed areas.
9 Agricultural subsidies (Federal agricultural assistance programmes now total $6 billion per annum).
10 Federal and state installations (offices, hospitals and other institutions, military establishments).
11 Contracts for military and aero-space and atomic energy programmes.
12 Conservation, power and waterway developments.

Land-use controls

Even though the regional pattern of land uses and values can be greatly influenced if not fairly precisely determined by correlated government activity in line with general policies and strategies, there is still need for a system of land-use controls to assure proper local area development.

Any system of development controls must be equally broad in its conception, and representative of metropolitan planning policies. In the United States there is great question as to whether any system of land-use controls will be administered in accord with such broad concepts as long as their administration rests completely with the most local level of government. Almost fifty years of experience with zoning administration at the local level have not had heartening results and, if anything, have created a vested interest that will be extremely difficult to dislodge. Experience in both nations indicates that it is not possible to establish a separate system of rules affecting land ownership based on the police power within the structure of a free-enterprise system. Effectively to overcome this obstacle, it would seem necessary and appropriate to base a system of controls on the power of eminent domain. For if the people want proper development should they not be willing to pay for it? Furthermore, there are increasing alternative sources other than land for private investment and speculation in our industrial economy.

The compensation and betterment aspects of the British Planning Act of 1947 were an experimental step in this direction which really never were given a full opportunity to operate since there were so many unforeseen obstacles and details of administration to be mastered within a short time. Perhaps it was the attempt to set the development charge at 100 per cent of the value increment which created the greatest difficulty and opposition. In any event, this experience did not disprove the need for financial incentives to bring about land development in the public interest. A simpler system more susceptible to uniform administration must be devised. In the United States, such a system might be based on a return to the localities of capital gains tax payments resulting from land-value increments.

Popular acceptance of any new system of land-use and value controls can only be achieved when the policies and strategies of metropolitan development which the system is designed to achieve are recognised by the public as necessary and desirable. Such recognition is likely to occur only if such policies and strategies are in tune with the context of our social, economic and political structure and the emerging forces which are reshaping this structure.

10

TRANSPORT AND LAND USE

Mr May's argument raised another question: which economic forces are capable of being harnessed by public investment to a planning strategy, and which are basic factors which the planner must accept as given if he wants his strategy to work? Planners might frustrate their own efforts to influence the form of regional development by taking dependent economic variables as given, no less than by treating economic constants as manipulable. This was the point emphasised by Mr Munby when he opened the next session, at which the seminar got down to a more detailed consideration of the relationship between transport and regional forms. His paper read as follows.

Transport both depends on the pattern of the activities it serves, and itself creates the pattern. Much trouble has arisen when both aspects have not been considered together. A very rough and exaggerated, but not entirely false, statement of the situation in Britain would be that the transport industry (including the Ministry of Transport, as a producer of transport media—trunk roads and motorways) has been solely concerned with serving other activities, whereas town planners have been concerned with moulding transport to produce the desired pattern of activities. The exception in the transport industry has been the promotional activities of railways (London Transport and British Railways) in the London region. An exception on the other side is the Buchanan Report, which, by and large, takes the activities of a city as given and considers how these activities can be served by modern means of transport. But on the whole the transport industry and the Ministry of Transport have been a conservative force, like the Board of Trade in its location of industry policy, whereas the town planning Ministry and the town planners have been a revolutionary force.

Even more revolutionary has been the impact of the motor vehicle. The last fifty years have seen its double effect: first, the shift from the railways and the horse-drawn vehicle to the public providers of motor transport; second, the shift from the public providers to the use of one's own vehicles (whether a firm's goods transport on its own account ('C' licences) or a person's private car). It is the second effect which has the most impact on the urban scene, and whose consequences have been largely ignored or underestimated until recently in Britain. But we do in fact know that we have to look forward within the next twenty years to a fantastic increase in the number of private cars (from $5\frac{1}{2}$ millions in 1960 to some 12 millions in 1970 and 19 millions in 1980; all vehicles from 9 to 18 to 27 millions).

The next ten to fifteen years are crucial for policy; the decisions made from now on will set the pattern of living in the twenty-first century, as we rebuild our city centres and inner rings, determine the sites for new towns and overspill, and decide on our motorways, ports, airports, and railway investment and disinvestment. Effectively we have no strategic plans, and little knowledge about many of the quantitative determinants. There are many pieces of tactical plans (Beeching for railways, Rochdale for ports, the Ministry of Transport's motorway schemes; the *ad hoc* programmes for the North-East and Central Scotland; the South-East Study; financial induce-ments to firms under Development Area legislation, etc.), but most of these assume the existence of a drift of policy. We have bits of knowledge about some of the costs and alternative advantages of different policies, but no one has brought all the studies together. There is, in general, no coherent policy on a coherent set of assumptions.

The historical background

The growth of our modern cities has been determined, or at least made possible, by the technical inventions of the public providers of mass transport —tram, bus, underground and electric railway. There is a rough absolute limit to the size of a city given by the time taken to reach the central employ-ment area (say an hour and a half's journey time). The growth of London from about 1900 to 1939 was the product of the uncontrolled enterprise of London's public providers of transport. Even of recent years they have not been entirely backward in determining shifts of population which the planners have had to accept.

Public providers of mass transport are almost all in agreement in every city that the town planners do not consult with them before they make decisions or take account of their problems and opportunities, and this in spite of most town planners' prejudices in favour of public over private transport. More often than not the planners have lost out as a result.

Not only the size, but also the pattern of the city's activities have been determined by transport. The concentration of activities in central business areas is the natural response to the technical opportunities of mass transport. In this respect the motor vehicle made no difference to the pattern already established or on the way to establishment as a result of the tram and electric railway so long as the motor vehicle was privately owned by only a small part of the population and most people travelled to work by public transport.

On the other hand the motor vehicle made a great deal of difference to the pattern of goods transport. Firms were no longer tied to railways or water transport with the horse delivery radius providing an effective barrier to dispersal. The lorry is a smaller unit relatively to the effective unit of demand than is the bus. Thus the lorry disperses production, whereas the bus collects people into streams, streams smaller than those required by rail transport, but still large in relation to centres of population and the pattern of transport flows they generate. As a result it is not altogether surprising that decentralisation of industry from urban centres both to the periphery and to other centres has tended to occur, though not on any large scale, and has been easier to stimulate than the equivalent dispersal of offices, services and 'tertiary' activities. As these latter have been the growing sectors of the economy the pressures towards centralisation and its concomitant suburban sprawl have grown precisely at the time when the new technical means (the private car) make it less necessary and less economic. The failure of town planners to realise the significance of office growth in the centre of London and of the government to take action until too late is without excuse.

The crisis of public passenger transport mounted in the fifties as private car ownership spread. It can be summarised in terms of the following facts. Public road passenger travel has steadily declined from a peak of nearly 51 billion passenger miles in 1953 to 42 billion in 1962. In London, the decline has been continuous since 1948 (and it applies to London Transport railways also[1]). Urban transport has lost more severely at the off-peak than at the peak, while peak flows have tended if anything to become more accentuated as a result of various economic and social changes. As a result the cost of public travel has gone up both absolutely and relatively to the cost of private travel.[2]

---

[1] London Transport road services from 9·1 billion passenger miles in 1948 to 5·7 in 1961; railways from 3·8 to 3·1 billions. On the other hand, total travel on British Railways reached its peak in 1957, and travel on the London lines of B.R. was higher in the early sixties than the early fifties (4·6 and 4·9 billion passenger miles in 1949 and 1961).

[2] The following price index numbers make it clear:

1962	(1953 = 100)
Bus and coach fares	155
Car prices	106
Running cost of vehicles	115
Consumer prices	127
Railway fares	167

End of 1962	(End of 1953 = 100)
London bus fares	170
Local authority buses (mostly urban)	159
All bus and coach fares	158

The shift to private transport would have occurred with the growth of car ownership, even if there had been no relative shift in costs, but the cost shift is not unimportant. The vicious spiral of less traffic—higher costs—worse services—still less traffic is inescapable in a situation where cars are used in the off-peak for journeys which were formerly by bus and where the proportion of journeys to work by private car increases even by one or two percentage points.[1]

The road and railway systems were allowed to decay up to 1954 as a result of deliberate government investment priorities. What road building had taken place in the twenties and thirties outside towns had done little, if anything, to alter the pattern of roads inherited from the Romans and the Middle Ages. Within cities the major alterations to pre-existing patterns came before the motor age from the exertions of High Victorian civic enterprise. (In London the despised and corrupt Metropolitan Board of Works (1855-89) did more than the LCC and the Metropolitan Boroughs in all the years from 1889 to 1939; pre-World War I Kingsway is the most notable achievement of the LCC. After World War II the Ministry allowed the major road reservations proposed in Abercrombie's Plan to be built over, without any alternative plans being accepted.)[2] The cessation of road building did not lead to any concentration of effort on planning and preparation of schemes. If anything the authorities were even worse prepared in 1954 than in 1945.

---

1 Between 1951 and 1961, the number of persons travelling to central London between 7 a.m. and 10 a.m. rose from 1,175,000 to 1,323,000. The private car share increased from 3 per cent to 7 per cent, while the number travelling by bus fell absolutely and the share fell from 25 per cent to 16 per cent. This comparatively small shift was quite enough to produce almost insoluble problems. (The rail share, notably British Railways, increased also, and there was a small increase in the share coming in by cycle.)

2 'Between the completion of Kingsway/Aldwych in 1905 and the outbreak of war in 1939 substantial road works in central London were mainly concerned with the river crossings (six Thames bridges being rebuilt, one widened, and the Rotherhithe Tunnel constructed), widenings of main roads in connection with the tramway system, arterial roads mainly on the South-Eastern outskirts, and part of the South Circular Road.'

The London Plan proposals were for an A-ring about 1½-2 miles from Charing Cross and a B-ring about 3-4 miles out; 'the latter road was considered to be the principal ring road'. 'The Ministry of War Transport favoured the A-ring motorway and relegation of the B-ring to sub-arterial status . . . The Government in May 1950 decided that the project (for the A-ring) should not proceed . . . Because of extensive redevelopment, particularly on the north side of the river, that has taken place since the proposal was considered in 1948 the original alignment is no longer practicable . . . Planning advantages suggested for the B-ring motorway were that it would pass through . . . districts (which) would, in any case, require priority in post-war reconstruction because of war damage and obsolescence. These arguments would not be so valid today when much redevelopment has taken place.'
(*Report of the Committee on London Roads*, Cmnd. 812, 1959, para. 10, and Appendix III, paras. 1, 3, 4, 21, 24.)

Since 1954, a motorways plan has been initiated with a programme of 1,000 miles to be built by the early 1970s, based largely on assessments of the actual incidence of congestion (or savings in time as a result of its removal) and thus largely perpetuating the London-dominated pattern of activity. The Ministry of Transport has thus taken over the role which the railway builders played in the nineteenth century, but has been quite insensitive until recently to the promotional aspect of its activities, of which the railway builders of the last century were well aware.

Concentration of attention on the stale problem of road and rail co-ordination and its solution in terms of autonomy and commercial freedom for the various units has begun to restore some economic sense to transport thinking, but has diverted the attention of the transport planners away from the fields where co-ordination of major decisions can produce large economic and social gains, as in planning growth points in relation to motorways, railway concentration and port investment. Cost—benefit studies rightly initiated in relation to major transport investment (M.1, Victoria Line, electrification of G.N. suburban lines, etc.) may be an excuse for avoiding major decisions which will in any case be inevitable long before an adequate framework for cost-benefit analysis on the scale required can be worked out. The publication of the results of the London Traffic and Travel Survey may provide a framework of basic knowledge for much metropolitan planning, as the Buchanan Report provides a basic strategic appraisal of the problems. But no clear policy or pattern of action has yet emerged.

The technical background

1 *Inter-urban transport*

a) *Goods* We know very little about the flows of traffic about Britain; the major source of information is the Beeching Plan (both for road and rail). The vast bulk of all goods other than coal and iron and steel go by road. But goods traffic only represents about a third of all traffic on inter-urban roads and its share is likely to fall.[1] The motorway plan, which is required in any case for passenger cars, will meet the needs for goods transport at the same time. There is thus no need to be much concerned with goods traffic in the overall pattern of development. Further, transport costs for most industries are so small a part of total costs in a country so small as Britain that they make little difference to location policies.

---

[1] The Hall Report calculated that heavy goods traffic (each vehicle counted as three passenger cars) represented 27 per cent of total inter-urban road traffic in 1960, and would be 22-4 per cent in 1970 and 23-6 per cent in 1980. Vans accounted for 8 per cent in 1960, and would fall to 6-7 per cent in 1970-1980. Together they represented 36 per cent in 1960, 29-31 per cent in 1970 and 30-2 per cent in 1980.

But we have not got a national motorway network and it will be many years at the present rate of progress before we do have one. Priorities in the building of motorways can therefore have a determining effect on location decisions, and co-ordination of these plans with plans for regional development, whether we are thinking of the overall growth of different regions or the inter-urban pattern within any given region, will be most important. Without such co-ordination, the pattern of development may be determined willy-nilly by the Ministry of Transport's road division.

b) Passengers The normal flows of passengers between regions and cities are not a major determining factor in planning policies. The one exception is the flow of commuters between urban units within a larger region. One possible pattern of development which is likely to develop in certain areas is commuting from villages or small towns into larger towns, or between urban units forming a constellation of activities. If we are to preserve green belts and limit the size of certain towns, such a development will be inevitable in certain cases, e.g. Oxford, where the labour for the motor industry will no doubt continue to be drawn from surrounding villages. Such a system meets many social needs, but requires an appropriate transport policy. It is not always clear that railway closures (e.g. in the Buxton case) are well related to such developments.

2 *Intra-urban transport*

a) Goods Again the major flows are passenger, but the problems of goods traffic are by no means unimportant. There are questions of the location of factories, warehouses, markets, railway stations, and other large generators of goods traffic; there are also problems of delivery to shops and other final consumption points. It seems likely that, in the latter case at least, we will need to make some radical changes in our arrangements, which will vary according to the size of cities and the kind of traffic plans developed for them. It might, for instance, be necessary in some cases to break bulk at the outskirts and organise deliveries to particular streets or shops.

b) Passengers The major problems arise from the journey to work. Most of the heavy generators of goods traffic will also be heavy generators of passenger traffic, though the converse is not necessarily true (e.g. offices). Thus the planning of location of work places in relation to transport will usually be dominated more by the passenger problem than by the goods problem. The same is true of the other activities of cities (shops, entertainments, housing), which generate traffic.

The fundamental issues revolve round two factual matters: the amount of space required for transport purposes with any given pattern of activities and any given form of transport, and the cost of transport involved in any such given pattern (including the cost of space). The work of Smeed has given us some idea of some of the factors determining space requirements for the journey to work, while the Buchanan Report suggests some of the broad magnitudes involved. But we know little of the alternative transport costs for different patterns in cities of different kinds and sizes.

But even with extensive knowledge of these factual matters, we would still be far from a knowledge of what an optimum would involve. Minimising the cost of transport will not provide an optimum. An increasing use of transport (with more cost and more space devoted to it) may maximise some other aim of industry or people. Thus firms may want to increase transport costs of goods in order to gain economies of scale and the same applies to drawing labour from a distance; people will want to minimise some combination of rent, cost of travel to work and time spent on travel, quite apart from other, non-measurable factors. What we want to know is what arrangements of cities will produce the optimum combination of all these factors. Even if non-measurable factors in the long run are more important than the cost ones, costs are still relevant (e.g. the Buchanan law that more traffic facilities can be provided within a given environmental standard if more is spent). If we ignore costs, as all too often town planners do, we are likely to make a worse decision that we would do otherwise.

There is a further factor of considerable importance. *If* all costs were borne as they are incurred by those who benefit from them, then it would be possible to act on the basis of actual behaviour as highway enquiries tend to do. But they are not, notably in the use of roads in congested conditions, under-charging for parking space, and the way firms shift the inconveniences they cause onto others, notably their employees. Thus to assume, as the Buchanan Report does, that a transport plan must meet the given distribution of activities in a city is to plan for something less than the optimum. Partly this is because the activities will re-adapt themselves as the transport situation alters, at the very least because, as in the Leeds case, much less space is left for other than transport requirements, if transport requirements in the motor age are met even to a limited degree; but, more importantly, because the present activities are located where they are because people do not pay the full amount of the costs they cause to be incurred.

Where do we go from here?

Cities will have to adapt themselves to a fully motorised world; the city problem is the one really big issue. But there are several forms of adaptation, none uniquely relevant to cities of all kinds and sizes. A number of different patterns need to be explored for different cities, both existing and new:

Smaller cities

1 The smallish city with an historic centre, which has to be preserved with a

minimal possible relocation of activities. The centre may be entirely restricted to pedestrians with car parks and access for loading and unloading on the periphery.

2 There may be partial restriction of the centre for pedestrians, and the use of the price mechanism (either parking charges or electronic systems of charging for the use of the roads) to limit traffic to a chosen level.

3 The same result may be achieved by careful planning of bus-only routes.

4 The pattern may make possible a fully motorised plan with motorways, car parks, etc. The public using these facilities may be ready to pay for them.

Larger cities

1 A fully motorised plan may be possible with reallocation of activities, so that shopping, entertainments and workplaces are not all located centrally or in concentrated areas.

2 A fully motorised plan for all but the main journey to work to the centre. This may be achieved by subsidy to buses or undergrounds, direct control of private traffic at peak hours (limiting certain streets to buses only) or the use of stringent financial pressures.

3 A mainly bus and taxi city with marginal use of cars.

In designing new cities, we can design them in ways to achieve any of these types. What we want to see are fully worked out studies of alternative types of development so that we can compare the costs and the overall pattern which emerges. Thus we want studies of the costs of building a city of a given size and of using it, *a*) with no use of cars within the city, but easy access from private garages outwards and easy access inwards for visitors, *b*) the fully motorised city, and *c*) the partially motorised city planned for a limited use of cars (e.g. for everything except the journey to work) with the appropriate means of limiting cars built into the design. Each of these types would have to be studied in relation to different patterns of activity (notably whether concentrated in the centre or more scattered, and for different densities of residential development).

With such models behind us and with the results of comprehensive traffic surveys such as the London one, we would be able to make a better choice of the actual alternatives that confront any given city. In practice, except for the entirely new city, the pattern of the past is heavily dominant. But, it must be stressed again, there is no evidence that the past configuration of activities is more inflexible than the geographical and economic factors which limit the possibilities of completely new road patterns. On the contrary, many activities are only marginally located where they are, and the obsolescence of buildings often requires redevelopment. The major stumbling-block to more comprehensive reassessment of city patterns is the need to take big decisions affecting many activities together; the limit is more the economic knowledge and imagination of town planners and the narrowly financial boundaries to local government action than the essential economics of the situation.

Introducing his paper, Mr Munby insisted that planning and transport could not be analysed separately. Transport affected development and vice versa. In the comprehensive analysis of planning and transport we should take two factors as given: on the one hand, human desires and values, and on the other the primary economic forces, of which transport was one. But we must be very clear exactly what these economic forces were. The growth of offices in London, for example, was only a secondary economic force dependent on a given transport pattern and a given pricing policy. The primary economic forces were the factors which, given a price structure, produced a particular pattern—the fundamental facts of technology and cost structure, not the particular policies that resulted from a particular conglomeration of economic circumstances.

Illustrating the ways in which comprehensive plan-making could go wrong if the wrong factors were taken as given, Mr Munby took as his first example the Buchanan Report, which, he said, was admirable strategically, except that it assumed the present location of city activities and then asked what we should do with the traffic arising from them. It might be very much less costly to move the activities than to build urban motorways.

Another example was the traffic-engineering approach—about which Britain had a lot to learn from the Americans. This approach tended to extrapolate trends and to take insufficient account of the amount of additional traffic which was itself produced by the building of motorways. This was a possible danger in the British traffic surveys, for which American consultants and techniques were being used.

A third example was the Beeching Report. Dr Beeching's brief had been to make the railways pay: he had been given no objectives in terms of town planning, regional development and the growth of cities. His report had said all the right things about this, but had proposed the closure of lines which would probably be important in relation to overall planning objectives.

A fourth example was the still more masterly Rochdale Report—the first analysis we had ever had of the ports in Britain—whose authors specifically said that they had to assume the continuation of present trends in population growth. One of their proposals was to increase the capacity of the port of Southampton, and this had now been tentatively agreed to in the South-East Study. It might be that if the Rochdale Committee had been told in general terms what was to happen in the country as a whole they would still have come up with the same answer. Nevertheless there was a fallacy here, for the South-East Study had been based on a different set of assumptions.

A final example was the motorways plan which had quite clearly been designed by Ministry engineers in relation to existing trends, and had taken very little account of future possibilities for the redistribution of population among the different regions. This plan was now taken as the basis for regional planning. All this showed that in many fields there was a failure to make any really comprehensive analysis or to see the interrelationships of crucial factors. This was not the right way for planning to proceed.

As to the extent to which the form of urban redevelopment should be based on a redistribution of present activities or on increased provision for the private car or public transport, it was very clear that the answer depended on the size of the city. There was no one pattern: we must think in terms of experiment and of different solutions for cities of different sizes. We knew, for example, that the larger the city the smaller the proportion of private cars commuting to central areas. Whatever the solution might be, the important thing was to see that the planners made a quantitative approach to the pattern of development and that they used all the proper tools. The Liverpool Plan might be a perfectly good one, but it must be thought through from the major strategy right down to the tactics, Mr Munby concluded. 'If you are going to build a central motorway that will cater for just so much traffic, you must be quite sure that you limit the traffic to the capacity of the road, provide just the right amount of car parking and use all the tools that are now available—traffic-engineering tools, planning solutions (blocking up roads), pricing solutions (charging for road usage and car parks) and fiscal solutions (taxing central offices)—to ensure that the thing is coherent and makes sense in terms of what is planned for.'

The second paper on this topic was contributed by Mr Harris. Speaking from five years' association with the Pennsylvania-Jersey Transportation Study—a large and pioneering exercise in the planning of metropolitan transport in relation to land use—he said he regarded transportation as subordinate to the structure of the urban region. His paper continued:

Essentially, the urban setting improves the access of citizens to a variety of opportunities for consumption, recreation, education and employment, and of businesses and institutions to patrons, customers, audiences, employees, and suppliers. Since the frequency of these contacts varies, and since activities of different types have many different minimum sizes and frequencies of occurrence, there is a tendency for urban regions to be complex and highly structured, with a hierarchical arrangement of sub-centres. There is an apparent desire on the part of planners to improve and heighten this structuring of the metropolitan area, but their efforts in this direction seem somewhat blunted by the incremental growth of conurbations and by increased individual mobility. I believe that a more strongly structured metropolitan development with greater emphasis on relatively self-contained sub-centres is sound. I also believe, however, that current new town experiments are far too modest in the size of sub-centres which they attempt to create. It appears likely that centripetally organised sub-centres with populations of over a quarter of a million will be necessary to provide any very large range of consumer choice and choice of jobs. Such centres must also contain a great diversity of housing, and in the United States we are unable to provide an adequate volume of housing for the lower-income groups in a new community. Without very large sub-centres, the decentralisation of selected major city-centre functions will prove extremely difficult.

Transportation planning as presently conceived can probably not play any very highly effective role in bringing such large sub-centres into existence. It further seems unlikely to me that present urban planning tools, especially in the United States, have adequate affirmative content for this purpose. If speed is required, and it seems desirable, Draconian measures would probably be required to provide sufficiently diverse employment in a large sub-centre to ensure that it would be relatively self-contained and of sufficient size to continue successful growth. In the absence of such affirmative development policies and programmes, transportation planning will be constantly required to attempt solutions to the insoluble problem of servicing a metropolis which is highly centred on a single core area.

In the realm of planning strategies I believe, of course, that all planning powers should be co-ordinated so as to enforce and hasten development in desired directions. This statement leaves open many questions as to what powers are available for use and what are the desired directions. It appears to me, however, that we are presently woefully ignorant of the long-term effects of present policies. If we assume that the direct effects of planning actions are their only effects, that the effects of policies are additive, or that people will behave as predicted, we are, I believe, making serious mistakes. I feel that transportation planning techniques as developed in the United States offer considerable promise for improving our predictions of future developments under various policy assumptions. If so, we may have a means of making paper experiments with policies which are too slow or too expensive to experiment with on the ground. Such experimentation would be, in my opinion, a most important part of planning strategy.

It seems likely that the quantity and quality of transportation services have effects of overwhelming importance in the determination of land values. I hope that Nathaniel Lichfield and others will be in a position to comment on this important aspect of transportation cost-benefit analysis. Since the lowering of rents through transportation improvements would take from the landlord what it gives to the renter, these benefits may be mainly redistributive, but they are not unworthy of consideration.

It is now appropriate to make a few general comments on transportation policy and the major factors which lie behind its formulation. The most important of these, as I have remarked, is overall planning policy, and in the absence of adequate overall planning, transportation planning is apt to become responsive to demand rather than to demand reformulated through a plan, and it is apt to attempt to satisfy ultimate needs in a sub-optimising fashion.

One of the prime postulates of transportation planning and of urban planning in general must, I believe, be that mobility is very highly desired by the population in general. I believe that this desire is only now beginning to become very evident in Britain, and may still be held in check by existing patterns of family life and occupational immobility. The extent to which these desires should as a matter of overall policy be allowed to grow and be satisfied deserves very serious consideration. In forming our opinions we should, I believe, be very careful not to deny to others the mobility which we personally have or for which we are able to provide adequate substitutes by reading, personal contact, and the organisation of our home and professional existence —substitutes which may not be generally available.

We are not, I feel, fully justified in taking the position that public transportation provides a form of mobility which is identical with that provided by the family automobile or other personal vehicle. The comfort and convenience is frequently substantially lower in public transportation, and the cost for the numbers of people engaged in family activities is apt to be substantially higher.

The satisfaction of the public desire for mobility implies movement and movement occupies space. In our crowded urban environment, the accommodation of increased movement is egregiously expensive. We should be aware, however, that the terminal accommodations for vehicular movement are far more demanding than the accommodations for the movement itself. It seems likely, moreover, that the carrying capacity of well-designed freeways per lane per hour could be increased by a factor of ten to twenty were it not for the need to put up the vehicles at the end of the trip. The parking requirements for large vehicular movements seem likely to me to bomb out large sections of existing central business districts, so that the tight array of inter-related activities can no longer exist. Thus, the central cities may have a choice only between two modes of demise. Either they may cease to function as before, or they may continue to function and be inaccessible by broadly acceptable means of transportation.

From a consideration of the inherent dilemmas in the problems of mobility and transportation in crowded areas combined with the consumer preferences for individual transportation systems, I am coming to believe that, while the individually owned vehicle is here to stay, the private automobile in its present form is already obsolete. There is no easy way to pre-figure the technological revolutions which lie in the immediate future. It is quite likely, indeed, that their advent will be considerably delayed unless very considerable public resources are devoted to the research and innovation which the producers of conventional means of transport are unwilling to undertake. Meanwhile, much present policy must, I believe, be regarded as a stopgap designed to preserve what must be preserved until the future is more clearly visible.

The preservation of existing central business areas probably demands some selective decentralisation which can be achieved only through an overall process involving the creation of new sub-centres. In many areas, this decentralisation would be greatly assisted, as it has been in the United States, by a marked improvement in telephone facilities and other means of com-munication which can replace face-to-face contact. I believe that every effort should be made to preserve the existing compact character of selected centres through the provision of public transportation, preferably grade separated, and through the diversion of vehicular traffic. Advanced tech-nological means for expediting pedestrian movement should by no means be neglected. Combined forms of transportation (such as the American 'park and ride') should be encouraged and facilitated. In spite of the combined effect of all these measures, it will prove impossible to achieve higher levels of mobility without some serious dislocations and modifications of existing arrangements. While it is desirable to display considerable caution in the formulation of overall policy, considerable boldness will be necessary in the final design and effectuation of its components. In effect, urban transportation policy in the United States has become far more conservative than might be considered desirable because a basic conservatism at the overall policy level has been overlaid by a dilatory, ineffectual, and opportunistic attitude towards policy effectuation.

Opening the discussion on these two papers Mr Harris said he noticed a curious ambivalence among planners in dealing with questions of economics. On the one hand many felt that economics were not the ultimate consideration, while on the other hand they were continually running up against economic questions, defined in the most general sense of the allocation of resources to serve human needs. He thought we should not be ashamed of taking an economic view of many of these problems, and this he proposed to do.

One could directly affect the lives of people in a metropolitan area through the costs of transportation and housing. He completely accepted Mr Munby's point about the interrelation of transportation and land-use planning. He also agreed that, at a certain level, the Buchanan Report was a very poor guide to comprehensive planning. At the small scale it showed a marvellous insight into the problems of the direct physical relationship between transportation and land use and into the way in which stationary and moving uses interacted with each other. The framing of the problem in terms of access and environment was extremely well done and could provide a fruitful basis for elucidating problems at the lower end of the scale. But if one looked at, for example, the treatment of Leeds one could not fail to be aghast at the discussion, for two reasons.

First, the transportation-planning techniques used were not the best, but secondly—and far more important—the report included the very simple statement (which probably meant nothing to most of its readers) that 'we apply a growth factor of 2·33 per cent': it built into the land uses of Leeds for the year 2010 exactly the same pattern that existed in 1960. This was patently preposterous. In the first place, Leeds could not grow to that scale with its present transportation system, and a new transportation system on anything like the scale suggested for the area would in itself call for a tremendous relocation of land uses. In the second place, any conscious planning activity would try to unscramble the mess which was present-day Leeds.

On the question of mobility and opportunity, Mr Harris thought it was still an open question how much opportunity the average British citizen needed in relation to jobs, entertainment, education, recreation, etc. We should speak rather of a 'spectrum' of people, some of whom would need a great deal of opportunity and some little. It might be that the number of people who could comfortably live in the new towns, with their somewhat restricted opportunities for access to the rest of the metropolitan area, was a perfectly reasonable slice off the lower end of the spectrum. But we needed to know more about the shape of the distribution.

The role of the transportation system in the movement of people was largely to give access to opportunities. While we might succeed in redistributing employment opportunities so that population and employment were dispersed together, there would still be a certain number of people who would not be satisfied with the opportunities in their immediate vicinity and who would therefore wish to travel to other opportunities. This was not a whimsical wish, nor one that was promoted by the provision of expressways: it was a basic and important need in a growing and dynamic society. Consequently the potential volume of traffic might not be reduced as far as was generally assumed by the redistribution of employment opportunities and population in the correct proportions.

One could think of the interaction of transportation and regional forms in terms of alternatives of many types: alternatives in the size, location and spacing of new towns; alternatives in the size, location, spacing and mixture of transportation facilities; alternatives in the distribution and utilisation of open space; and alternatives in pricing policy. The multiplicity of these alternatives made their possible combinations very numerous, complex and difficult to analyse. Transportation engineering in the United States, by way of metropolitan-area transportation studies, had enabled us to analyse some of these possibilities through the development of 'systems engineering'. But one could not rely on the traffic engineer to apply systems engineering to their analysis, and it was wrong to disregard alternatives through fear of making the problem too confusing. Planners, like architects, should have no difficulty in working out a whole group of alternative combinations of factors: their difficulty was that they had no way of finding out directly which solution would be most successful from the functional and aesthetic points of view.

It was very dangerous to eliminate possible choices one after another by saying: 'we cannot do this because we are expected to locate industry in the North, we cannot do this because it will cost too much, and we cannot do this because it violates the green belt, etc.' This kind of thinking was a research analogue of 'muddling through': it prevented the planner from arriving at new combinations which when put together in an imaginative way suddenly made a great deal of sense. The problem was how to tell whether these things really were sensible. We were dealing with such a complex and difficult set of interactions that it was very hard to tell.

'I suggest', Mr Harris concluded, 'that the techniques of computer simulation, which are being developed for the testing of weapon systems and complex transport systems, or for operational research in industry, could well be applied to the testing of the interactions between the major elements and components—population groups and transportation facilities—in the existing metropolitan area, for which we can sketch possible future patterns of development. With these techniques we can form rough, but nonetheless very informative, ideas about the levels of utilisation of different facilities, about the disparity between demand and supply of buildings, of sites of different types and of different locations, and perhaps even about the rent levels which would be produced by the mould into which we pour the activities we want to see going on in a particular metropolitan area.

'This kind of tool, which is still not fully developed, can be of great use to planners as a way of manipulating the environment which is much less costly and which involves fewer serious mistakes than passing regulations and putting up buildings. The experience of working with this type of tool gives the planner a great deal more insight into the way in which the problem has to be formulated and the way in which the parts of the problem interact. I am not suggesting that the computer is smarter than the planner, but I am suggesting that the computer can deal with a great deal more complexity, and can follow through to its conclusion faster than a planner can. One builds into this kind of thing many assumptions which may be wrong: this danger must be watched out for. But I think this system can not only lead to a much better understanding and a much better evaluation of alternatives, but can also point the way to improvements in plans that have already been drawn up.'

Coming to the defence of Buchanan, Mr Bor asked what else he could have done—short of re-planning all the cities he considered. He had not proposed solutions: he had only shown what would be required if Leeds retained its present land-use pattern. But this raised the question of the extent to which central-area activities would have to be relocated in order to achieve 'full motorisation' in a large city. Mr Bor himself doubted whether the most radical relocation could achieve more than a marginal increase in accessibility—and he did not see how, given the present legislative protection of existing-user rights, British planners could hope to bring about any major relocation of such heavy traffic generators as office uses: it would involve a financial commitment that could not possibly be contemplated. All they could do was try to shift the emphasis in future development.

Mr Wells agreed that even if some kind of funding arrangement could get over the financial difficulty, Britain could not afford the sheer destruction of usable space or the labour and materials needed to replace it. But Professor Self thought Britain could achieve a great deal in the way of relocation merely by reinforcing spontaneous trends, if only its public policies all pulled together in that direction; instead, the effects of Britain's new town and industrial dispersal policies were being cancelled out by its road and transport pricing policies and by its subsidies for high-flat construction, all of which encouraged concentration in city centres. Mr Senior agreed with Mr Bor that Buchanan could not be blamed for taking the present location of uses for granted; what worried him was that Buchanan had also taken for granted the present price structure of road usage, which could not conceivably last much longer. He was concerned lest this price structure, which involved a very heavy subsidy on car-commuting, was also being taken for granted in the land-use-transportation studies now being made as the basis for the future planning of all Britain's conurbations, where the pattern of road use was bound to be radically altered when the car commuter was no longer subsidised.

Mr James, while admitting that British planners were inexperienced in the techniques and methodology described by Mr Harris, found a great deal of this discussion unrealistic in view of the large number of variables involved, and particularly of the amount of money involved. It would take Britain forty years to begin to produce the kind of motorway network that would satisfy the long-term needs of its large towns. What we did know was that certain roads were essential now in relation to functions that were bound to continue in their present locations for a very long time. How, he asked, could one take account of all the variables when one could not put an order of magnitude upon them? Or, if one could, what margin of error would there be in the resulting pattern when one knew one could put in only one or two roads over the next ten or twenty years?

Mr May asked whether the difficulty arose from the fact that in Britain (unlike America) public expenditure had to be shared among many types of development besides roads and housing; but Mr Tankel pointed out that this only increased the need for doing a systems analysis to find a rational basis for allocating public investment. Professor Rapkin, on the other hand, still had much confidence in the 'handicraft' method of observing where new activities were going and either facilitating this movement by making proper accommodation available or, if it was heading for an area where land-use conflicts would be abrasive, trying to stop it and induce it to go elsewhere. This did not mean that systems analysis, which tried to view the whole region globally, should be ignored; but by the time we had worked out the long-term implications of a wide variety of alternatives, many of the things we wanted to prevent would already have happened. We should therefore work at both levels simultaneously.

Dr Lichfield did not think Mr Harris's points were answered by saying that the exercise was complicated and difficult, or that Britain had limited resources, or that there were other severe limitations on what British planners could do. The fact remained that the typical British planning process was insufficiently sophisticated to deal with a problem as complex as city planning was now recognised to be. Somehow Britain must devise a planning system that saw the region as a whole, instead of being preoccupied with the balance sheet of a particular project, or with its effect on the rateable value of an area; and the computer did provide the opportunity for such an overall view. The South-East Study approach, by contrast, was to point out a series of trends and then take some kind of sensible political-administrative decision as to the extent to which it was possible to influence them in one direction or another.

Mr Harris replied that if the South-East Study had been set up in terms of a number of alternatives—impracticable though certain aspects of each alternative might seem—this might have led to the discovery of lines of approach and combinations of measures which had not previously been considered feasible, but which, because of their great pay-off, might prove much more feasible than what had actually been proposed. In any case, in the process of doing this the planners would come to understand much more intimately the interrelationships of the factors with which they were dealing, and would thus have more knowledge to go on when they came to deal with a similar problem in another part of the country. The alternative was to wait years for plans to work themselves out on the ground and then try to rectify their mistakes—by which time many of the alternative possibilities which now existed would have been utterly foreclosed by policy decisions.

The Pennsylvania-Jersey Transportation Study, on which he was working, would for the first time in America pull the planning of transportation out of transportation-systems engineering and put it into the context of metropolitan-systems engineering, which meant that it would make transport planning part of land-use planning rather than an independent force. It had been found that in the American context there were strong limits on the variability of behaviour tendencies. The average number and distribution of family trips was fairly well fixed, though individual families might make many more or less. The same applied to people's choice between the use of cars and of mass transportation in any given conditions of density, availability of services and so on—and most of these were circumstances which the British planner could manipulate. If they were subject to manipulation he ought to know what the consequences of manipulating them would be. It was only in the last five years that the American Federal Government had begun to show a strong interest in mass transportation and to try to take the first steps towards co-ordinating it with highway planning.

Mr James replied that the South-East Study had been seriously limited by the fact that no motorways could at this stage be added to the initial thousand-mile programme without subtracting from it elsewhere. As time went on and money became available, progressive additions might be made, making it possible to open up such areas as East Anglia for development. In any case the opportunities for changing by this means the distribution of population in the South-East would be very small within the period (up to 1981) which was the basis of the Study. This was a fact of life. The possibilities of the Severn Estuary, the Humber and parts of East Anglia should be considered in relation to the further large increase in population that was expected during the last twenty years of this century. One by-product of the Study had been that the Ministry and London Transport had got together to try and solve the problem of accommodating the future increase in commuter travel on suburban railways, with the result that means had been found of doing so at about a tenth of the cost of the large-scale new works that had previously been thought necessary for this purpose.

Mr Ash harked back to Mr Harris's suggestion that the opportunities offered to residents in Britain's new towns were limited. He welcomed discussion of the fact that the new towns had been planned on certain assumptions as to what was the desirable level of opportunities for their inhabitants. 'My own hunch', he added, 'is that the present arrangement is about right for a very large proportion of our population. In other words I think by and large our people are not all that ambitious. Certainly when they marry and have children some of the steam goes out of them.' But he thought that to put the next batch of new towns as far out as the South-East Study suggested would deprive people of opportunities which they would wish to have. He also thought that in the last analysis the computer, however useful to the planner, was no substitute for a lively and open mind and a consensus as to what was meant by new urban forms.

Mr Harris agreed, adding that Britain's initial motorway programme had evidently been laid down outside the comprehensive land-use-transportation context, and was to be condemned on that account. He went on to predict that planning would have no more influence on the subsequent motorway programme unless some such process as he had described was entered into during the next five or ten years; but he admitted that in spite of everything he found the South-East Study tremendously exciting and thought it would be a success. Professor Self confined his own praise of the Study to its positive side, describing its treatment of the commuter problem as its appalling negative side. He felt sure there were plenty of possible alternatives to spending huge sums on bringing in 200,000 more commuters in greater discomfort—such as steering office employment to sub-centres ten, fifteen or twenty miles from the centre of London—and that a cost-benefit analysis would prove them preferable, even if it meant 'rethinking the green belt'. Accepting the political difficulties to which his attention was drawn, he maintained that the possible alternatives should be realised and publicly discussed before decisions of this character were taken.

Mr Munby thought the trouble was that in Whitehall the government departments made decisions on a day-to-day basis within a certain political framework: the whole machinery of British government was rather incoherent and totally unsuited to the making of comprehensive long-term decisions. Ministers had to take decisions on an *ad hoc* basis because there were not enough experts in Whitehall: it had not been thought necessary to train them. The British government was, in fact, much less expert-oriented and research-oriented than the Federal Government or even the state governments in America. The real problem of city development was to establish and present the realistic alternatives, and he thought Britain could go further in this respect than the South-East Study had gone.

Professor Foley suggested that more stress be put on the development of a web of roads in the outer zone of the metropolitan region so as to 'pull the transportation round' to the point where certain nodes became very accessible from the rest of the outer ring. He thought this was the real revolution in the United States: a circumferential grid had been superimposed on the radial road system, with amazing effects on the volume of movement in the outer metropolitan areas. He was not convinced that in the South-East Study the British planners were proposing to put their transportation system positively to work in the sense of promoting peripheral accessibility. Mr James indicated that this was now under discussion with the county planning authorities.

In his concluding comments Mr Harris observed that a pricing policy for transport services (which was not subject to the same difficulties as a motorway programme) could at the same time provide funds for motorway construction, cut down motor traffic and improve social conditions. In America, too, planners' projections had been cut back at the insistence of public officials. This was a failure of politics rather than of technology, and raised the question of the relation between the planner as technician and as politician: should he subordinate himself to policy or take an active part in its formulation? 'In the long term,' said Mr Harris, 'we wish to influence very dramatic changes in our environment. But if we insist on limiting ourselves for political reasons to the available bundle of policies we cut ourselves off from influencing the future in the way it should be influenced.'

To this Mr James responded: 'Quite clearly, for us in Britain who are trying to do this job the social content of planning—the kind of Britain we want—is the real motivation behind the whole of our effort: to upgrade the physical environment, to see that people have decent homes, to reduce accidents on the roads, to see that we do not live in acute congestion. That is the heart and soul of planning.' It was extremely difficult, however, to separate out what planning was from the political responsibility of local and central government.

RECAPITULATION

The seminar concluded with a general session, opened by Professor Self, at which members drew attention to some of the salient points that had emerged from our discussions. Among these were the following:

Prof. Self: A basic change occurs when the scope of public action (comprising plans, controls and public investment) becomes dominant over the market—a position that has been reached in Britain, but not yet in America . . . As the scale and variety of public programmes grows, so does the need for integrating machinery—for planning strategies at the regional level to relate these programmes rationally one to another, and for forms of government to administer such plans. But the higher the level at which plans are made the more complex are the variables involved and the harder it becomes to achieve rationality . . . Regional strategies must reflect differences of cultural and aesthetic tradition as between, say, California and New York, but there are also cultural features common to Britain and America (such as a strong tendency for the distance between home and workplace to increase with rising wealth) which contrast sharply with the tradition of the Latin countries. Regional strategies must also keep up with shifting technological conditions and social demands, and this calls for more flexibility of mind than has often been shown in Britain; but this does not mean that a firm's own choice of location and estimate of operating costs should be the accepted criteria of economic efficiency . . . Disagreement as to the goals at which regional strategies should aim is inevitable, but most of us seem to want them to include the clearing of urban black spots, the focusing of new development, the retention of a green back-cloth, the upgrading of environmental quality and the reinforcement of the community spirit.

Mr Winnick: It is vital to grasp one significant difference between American and British planners as to the ideal form of the metropolitan region. Americans stress the great variety of choice and opportunity implicit in a concentrated arrangement of large, closely linked centres, while the British aim at a spread-out pattern of units, each just big enough to support a certain service—a theatre, for example, instead of a wide choice of theatres. The motive force of British planning strategy is fear of excessive size—anxiety lest any given settlement become too large. In America this concept is totally rejected. There is not a governor or a mayor of a county executive in the United States who would ever go on record as believing that his city or county was too big. The entire emphasis is still on boosting the size of the city.

Mr Thomas: To transpose the British situation into American terms you have to imagine California with a population of eighty millions instead of its present twenty millions. When that time comes will Americans still be unconcerned about size, and do we have to wait till then before America has effective centralised planning?

Mr Simon: It is not a question of being pro-size or anti-size: it is a question of regional structure. A metropolitan region can grow either as New York has grown or through new town building. America is more advanced in the techniques of traffic engineering, in the use of computers and in research, but when it comes to end-products the British are way ahead. If only American techniques and the use of Federal money for roads, rapid transit and urban-renewal programmes could be organised and co-ordinated by a philosophy of planning—totally lacking at present—who knows what we might not accomplish.

Prof. Mandelker: There is an inertia factor in the United States that should be emphasised. Any planning tool or mechanism we evolve has to travel a long political road through local, state and Federal legislation. Some of the inertia factors in the Federal framework prevent us from doing an effective job, and we should perhaps do better to pursue our goals through the state framework. But I do feel there is a problem in our failure to agree on a strategic rationale for the use of our tools.

Prof. Foley: Both of our countries have great difficulty in grappling with the possibilities for the positive structuring of the outlying parts of our large metropolitan regions. In both the Washington Year 2000 Plan and the South-East Study the main problem is what is to happen in these areas. It is not purely a problem of decanting population to relieve congestion at the centre, but one of finding a positive concept of what the city region of the future might be as we break away from the radial pattern based on rail transportation. I still find it amazing that in the South-East Study there is no discussion of how the transport system in the outlying areas might be redesigned to structure a web of relations among the communities it is proposed to establish there.

Mr Dyckman: We have not really answered the question whether we can freely structure the growth at the edges of metropolitan areas. We have noted the marginal differences in the techniques which our two countries have adopted in tackling this problem, but in substance we have essentially the same law, which is defensive about private property rights. We may have different attitudes towards bigness, mobility, permanence of settlement and the expansion of choice, but we share the same technology, and this is determining decisions to an extent we are reluctant to accept.

Mr Harris: Basically the whole problem is one of organising the large metropolitan area as a whole, whatever the culture, tastes and levels of income that may prevail now and in the future in any particular area. We have diverging practical problems about tools, techniques and goals, but this is the central problem and we all see it in very much the same way. It is possible that some large city in the United States may make a breakthrough in terms of governmental organisation and planning strategy that will enable it to manage the technology in a way that has a broad, popular appeal. If this were to happen, Americans are so pragmatic that many other cities might quickly follow that city's example. This is less likely to happen in Britain, where the central government is relatively strong and the cities themselves less free-standing.

Mr Winnick: Washington is the one city which at present could do this.

Mr Dyckman: California is one of the few states that is a genuine region. The state legislature's programme of regional studies represents, potentially at least, a remarkable commitment to planning by American standards.

Mr Tankel: Britain has been successful in neighbourhood planning (which is what the new towns essentially are) but its regional planning has failed, both on the inter-regional and on the intra-regional scale, because it is unnecessarily trying to push the market uphill. I see no point in trying to redistribute the growth of population and employment between regions. It is the design of the region that matters, not its size: it can be made to work at any size it could attain. Within the region the green belt policy and the idea of self-contained communities are not achieving their ostensible objectives. I am against these policies not because they involve public intervention, but because public intervention in these forms does not work.

Mr Wells: When Americans have reached the point where their many planning tools are combined in a rational machine they will have to face the issue of compensation and betterment—in relation, for example, to the use of site value as the basis of property taxation. American economists ought to be ready to deal with this problem, as British economists were not—which is one reason why Britain, after twenty years of thinking about it, has still not solved it.

Mr Slayton: The tools available in America will not be really useful until we have a government mechanism in which they can be operated. This is not a matter of assembly but of organisation.

Dr Lichfield: American planners have to struggle with an archaic set of tools, because the planning mechanism has no appeal for the American mind, but they make tremendous progress when they get down to what the American development machine understands. The future of American planning may lie in forgetting the sort of machinery Britain has tried to build up and getting behind the large spending programmes that really make planning tick.

Mr May: Neither tools nor machinery are indispensable to the success of planning, nor can they ensure it. There are not many regional or metropolitan problems that cannot be taken care of through *ad hoc* agencies, and no metropolitan machinery can take care of the attitude of metropolitan people. Unless the opinions, prejudices and desires of the people are expressed in the plan they will work on any governmental system to limit the use of whatever controls may be devised. There will be no improvements in our environment until there is a general awareness of more important values than those now guiding us.

Mr Munby: Britain has not got very far in using the entrepreneurial and managerial abilities of private developers. When it comes to the operational job of implementing the strategy we must ensure that the resources of the private sector are used in a co-ordinated way. This may be more difficult to achieve in Britain than in America because of the tradition that Whitehall keeps at arm's length from businessmen.

Winding up the seminar, Mr Gutheim said he was more conscious of the things that had been omitted from our discussions than of any clear-cut conclusions. We had failed to grasp the significance of America's abandonment, in its urban renewal, of the traditional low-density structure of its cities, in contrast to what was happening in the older, more crowded and obsolescent cities of Britain and Europe. On the other hand, the strength of America's East Coast urban belt lay in its remarkably fine suburbs, which formed a very clear model of the style of living that was increasingly attractive to the leisured and affluent American. More could have been said about the miserable way the resources squeezed out of Congress for rapid rail transport had been wasted on the subsidising of inefficient and unprofitable systems rather than used to create the bones of a regional structure, and about one of America's greater strengths—the work of its Outdoor Recreation Resources Review Commission in the fields of open space, leisure and the role of agriculture in the metropolitan region. Finally, we had looked at the present and at the far future, but had neglected the middle distance: the period about eight or ten years hence was a strategic area for planning thought.

APPENDIX 1

Extracts on the administration, powers and finance of new town development corporations from the report of the Ministry of Housing and Local Government for 1960.

Administration

The major responsibility for planning and building a new town is placed upon a development corporation appointed by the Minister. Each corporation consists of a chairman, a deputy chairman, and not more than seven other members.

The corporations appoint their own staff and are substantially independent of the Minister in their day-to-day work. But as they are wholly financed by the Exchequer their powers fall short of the 'freedom of action comparable with that of a commercial undertaking' which the Reith Committee[1] advocated. Thus their proposals for development require the approval of the Minister and the concurrence of the Treasury as 'being likely to secure for the corporation a return which is reasonable, having regard to all the circumstances, when compared with the cost of carrying out those proposals.'[2] This general formula gives the Minister and the Treasury a wide discretion. It does not require all development proposals to show a profit— some, indeed, by their very nature show a loss—but it is incumbent on the corporations to prepare their plans with proper economy and on a prudent and business-like basis. Within the limits imposed by the statute, however, the corporations enjoy a fair degree of independence.

The corporations have wide powers 'to secure the laying out and development of the new town . . . and to do anything necessary or expedient for the purposes of the town or for purposes incidental thereto'. Nevertheless the corporation does not replace or usurp the functions of the elected authority for the area and the normal functions of local government continue to be

[1] 'Interim Report', para. 9(5). *Report of the New Towns Committee 1946.*
[2] New Towns Act 1946, section 12(7).

exercised by the local authorities. But it was recognised that the provision over a relatively short period of time of all the services and publicly financed amenities which, in older towns, have been provided slowly over many years would throw too heavy a burden on the local authorities, especially in the early years while rateable value was building up. The corporations were, therefore, empowered to contribute towards the expenditure incurred by local authorities or statutory undertakers in the performance of their functions in the new towns.

The existence of a development corporation operating extensively in the area of a local authority or statutory undertaker is plainly a potential source of friction. There have been difficulties but in general these have been satisfactorily resolved, and there has been good co-operation with the local authorities, including the county councils. The latter have carried, among other things, the particularly heavy burden of providing the many new schools and colleges needed for the children in the towns.

Planning control

Development proposals from the corporations approved by the Minister after consultation with the local planning authority and other local authorities concerned are automatically granted planning permission by the Town and Country Planning (New Towns Special Development) Order, 1950 (S.I. 1950, No. 152). In the case of other development proposals within the designated area, the local planning authority is required to consult with the development corporation and if the two bodies are unable to reach agreement the application is referred to the Minister for decision.

Acquisition of land

The New Towns Act 1946 enables a development corporation to buy, by agreement or compulsorily, with the Minister's approval, any land within the designated area, and for certain purposes land outside the area. The general policy has been to buy land only as and when required for development and to reduce to a minimum any inconvenience to owners by negotiating terms and offering reasonable alternative accommodation wherever possible. Most purchases have been by agreement and there have been very few opposed compulsory purchase orders.

The Act also gives any landowner within the designated area the right, at any time after seven years from the date of designation, to require the development corporation to buy his land. This is a protection to owners who might otherwise find difficulty in selling their property on the open market, and the right has been extensively used. But not all the land within the designated areas has been, or will be, acquired. Particularly in those towns where there was a nucleus of existing development at the time of designation much remains and will remain in private hands.

In general the arrangements have proved satisfactory. No difficulties have arisen in making land available for the planned programme of development by the development corporation or their lessees, or by local authorities, statutory undertakers and other public bodies. In many cases the development corporation have sold or leased land to private builders for development in accordance with the programme.

Since the coming into operation of the Town and Country Planning Act 1959, current market value has been the basis of compensation for land bought by development corporations. But inside the designated area of a new town there is one important difference compared with elsewhere. In assessing compensation, the effect on the current market value of any existing or proposed new town development is disregarded. Thus, corporations do not have to pay for the development value which they themselves have created.

Finance

Advances to meet capital expenditure

Repayable loans The development corporations are financed by advances[1] made to them by the Minister to provide working capital and to enable them to defray expenditure. They are not allowed to borrow from any other source. The advances are repayable on terms approved by the Treasury and corporations are required to repay all such capital advances over a period of sixty years, by equal annual instalments of principal and interest combined.

Rate of interest The rate of interest is prescribed by the Treasury and was 3 per cent per annum when the first corporations were established in 1947. It rose steadily with the general rise in interest rates until the autumn of 1957 when it reached 6 per cent and has since fluctuated between that figure and 5 1/8 per cent. Most of the corporations had substantial advances at the lower rates, however, and the average rate of interest on all advances to all corporations up to 31 March 1960 was fractionally below 4 3/4 per cent, varying for individual corporations from just over 4 1/4 per cent to just under 5 1/8 per cent.

Grants In addition to repayable advances, the Minister can also make outright grants to development corporations under section 12(2) of the 1946 Act to enable them to defray expenditure other than capital expenditure. Under this section grants amounting in all to £446,725 were made towards the revenue deficits of development corporations in the first few years of their life—50 per

---

[1] The total authorised by Parliament was recently raised to £550 million.

cent of the deficit for the period to the end of the first complete year and 25 per cent for the second year. In addition, £988,806 of revenue expenditure during this initial period was capitalised and met from capital advances. Grants are also made under this section (in addition to the standard Exchequer housing subsidy) at a rate equal to one-third of the standard annual subsidy for every house built by the development corporation and not disposed of either freehold or for a lease-term longer than seven years. The total amount so paid for the whole period up to 31 March 1960 amounts to £2,699,535. The grants for the year ending 31 March 1960 amounted to £557,235 and this figure rises each year as more houses are built. The amount of standard housing subsidies payable to development corporations under the Housing Acts between 1947 and 31 March 1960 was £8,390,788. The housing grants and subsidies are at present running at the rate of about £615,000 and £1,780,000 a year respectively.

Other revenue

Apart from grants and housing subsidies, the corporation's revenue income consists of the rents from their houses, shops, factories and other property. To the extent that total revenue does not suffice to meet expenditure on revenue account, consisting of salaries and fees (other than those charged to capital as part of the cost of building and other works) and general office and administrative expenses, the deficit is carried forward and met by advances of working capital. At the beginning of each financial year, development corporaions are required to submit a budget to the Minister for approval, and within the approved budget figures they are not subject to detailed control over day-to-day expenditure.

APPENDIX 2

'Overspill' New Towns

	Year Designated	Original	December 1963	Target	Ultimate
			POPULATION		
For London					
Stevenage	1946	7,000	49,500	60,000	80,000
Crawley	1947	10,000	56,300	55,000	75,000
Harlow	1947	4,500	60,640	70,000	80,000
Hemel Hempstead	1947	21,000	58,700	63,000	80,000
Hatfield	1948	8,500	21,600	25,000	30,000
Welwyn Garden City	1948	18,500	37,000	42,000	50,000
Basildon	1949	25,000	58,000	80,000	100,000
Bracknell	1949	5,000	22,390	40,000	54,000
For Glasgow					
East Kilbride	1947	2,400	34,500	undecided	70,000
Cumbernauld	1956	3,000	8,350	,,	70,000
Glenrothes	1948	1,100	14,140	32,000	50–52,000
Livingston	1962	—	—	—	70,000
For Liverpool					
Skelmersdale	1961	6,000	6,000	70,000	80,000
Runcorn	1963	26,000	26,000	70,000	?
For Birmingham					
Dawley	1962	20,000	20,000	90,000	100,000+
Redditch	1963	35,000	35,000	70,000	?
For Tyneside					
Washington	1964	20,000	—	70/80,000	—

Others

Newton Aycliffe	1947	60	13,700	35,000	40,000
Peterlee	1948	200	14,400	24,000	30,000
Cwmbran	1949	12,000	32,000	45,000	55,000
Corby	1950	15,700	39,500	55,000	75,000

Employment 100,000 jobs in new factories
90,000 in services

Houses 135,000 completed by mid-1963

Schools 240 completed by mid-1963

INDEX